conversations with
remarkable **Native
Americans**

SUNY series, Native Traces

Gerald Vizenor and Deborah L. Madsen, editors

conversations with remarkable **Native Americans**

Joëlle Rostkowski

state university of new york press

Book cover: Tony Abeyta, *Totem*, collage, 2009.

Page iii: Tony Abeyta, *Tin Tintabulation*, Triptych (oil), 1997.

STATE UNIVERSITY OF NEW YORK PRESS
Albany, New York

Published by State University of New York Press, Albany

For information, contact State University of New York Press, Albany, NY
www.sunypress.edu

Production and book design, Laurie Searl
Marketing, Michael Campochiaro

Library of Congress Cataloging-in-Publication Data

Conversations with remarkable Native Americans / by Joëlle Rostkowski.
    p. cm. — (Native traces)
  Includes bibliographical references and index.
  ISBN 978-1-4384-4175-7 (hardcover : alk. paper) 1. Indians of North America—Biography. 2. Indians of North America—Civil rights. 3. Indians of North America—Government relations. 4. Indians of North America—Ethnic identity. 5. Indians of North America—Intellectual life. I. Rostkowski, Joëlle.
  E89.C66 2012
  323.1197'073—dc23   2011019510

10 9 8 7 6 5 4 3 2 1

In memory of Levi General, Deskaheh (Haudenosaunee),

who came to Geneva in 1923 to present his

REDMAN'S APPEAL FOR JUSTICE

to the League of Nations.

Contents

Acknowledgments

For my mother, Lucienne Ribert, who gave me my roots and my wings, and showed me the beauty of the world.

For my husband and traveling companion, Nicolas Rostkowski, managing partner of the Orenda Gallery, where Native artists are welcome.

For Edilou, student of art and budding artist, our daughter.

I am grateful to Gerald Vizenor and Deborah Madsen for their insights, encouragement and their interest in international research.

Special thanks to James Peltz and Laurie Searl for their faith in this book and to the SUNY production team for their friendliness and efficiency.

Thank you to the Remarkable Native Americans, whose voices are heard in this book, for their courage, creativity, and humor and for sharing with me some of their dreams.

In memory of my father, André Ribert,

None of our dreaming was in vain.

Jane Mendelsohn

Tragic wisdom and survivance

Deborah L. Madsen

The guiding principle of the Native Traces book series is the concept of *survivance*, developed by Gerald Vizenor and exemplified by Joëlle Rostkowski's conversations with a series of extraordinary Native Americans. Survivance is not a static object or method but a dynamic condition of historical and cultural survival and also of political resistance: an epistemology, an ontology, and an axiology. Survivance is the continual assertion of nonterritorial Native sovereignty, which the interviewees in this book describe as the condition of their lives as artists, writers, journalists, lawyers, and activists.

Survivance, as a structuring epistemological principle, is political, cultural, and aesthetic, a resistance and counterinterpretation that constantly seeks to expose the workings of dominant colonialist ideologies in the production of everyday meanings. Survivance refuses the easy acceptance of the "commonsense" interpretation of the world that supports what Aileen Moreton-Robinson calls the "possessive logic" of nation-state sovereignty.[1] Vizenor describes this interpretative resistance as the "unsaying" of the world and the corresponding effort to speak it "otherwise" in Native terms.[2] In this way, survivance counters the epistemology of disavowal that characterizes settler relations with Native peoples. Freud's concept of disavowal names a psychological process of simultaneous acknowledgment and denial, characterized by knowing what is actually the case but behaving as if it were otherwise. Disavowal is a defensive function that allows the rejection of some perception of reality because, if accepted as real, that perception would threaten the integrity of an existing worldview. In the context of U.S. settler colonialism, the history of Native dispossession is both acknowledged and denied, for example, in the official legal doctrines of "discovery" and "conquest" that regulate relations between the federal and tribal governments.

Survivance rejects the historical and cultural narratives that deny a Native sense of presence, a presence that preceded and endures despite colonial settlement. These narratives write Native communities into a condition of absence—a disavowed presence—and as perpetual victims lacking individual and communal agency. However, as Gerald Vizenor tells Joëlle Rostkowski in the interview published here, "The character of survivance creates a sense of native presence, a critical, active presence and resistance, over absence, historical and cultural absence, nihility and victimry."

Suzan Harjo expresses a common experience among the interviewees here when she tells how this character of survivance was articulated to her in her childhood by family and teachers who "told me that white people would try to break my spirit, just as they had twisted history. . . . I was always prepared for outsiders to try to make me and our Native peoples into lesser beings, and to resist them and to prevail."

The National Museum of the American Indian (NMAI) is an institution inspired by the sentiment of survivance. Indeed, the permanent exhibits are structured around the central assertion of ongoing Native presence and one of the installations, included in the permanent exhibit *Our Lives*, prominently displays Vizenor's definition of survivance. The NMAI presents visitors with a succession of survivance narratives that, like the stories told in the conversations presented here, testify to the falsity of dominant narratives that emphasize Native victimry and absence. As Richard West, the founding director of the NMAI, remarks in his interview, "We conceived a museum that was to become not only a cultural space but also a community center. To the consternation of some people it has asserted its difference, its specificity as a civic space where one is confronted not only with native objects but also with the native experience." This Native experience—this Native epistemology or worldview—is inseparable from the objects that constitute the museum's collection. West explains that "Objects tell a story. They have a language. To interpret the objects, you need to know the history of the communities and the meaning of the ceremonies. They sometimes have a spiritual dimension that exceeds their aesthetic value." This recognition of the epistemological power of survivance, enacted in the mission and structure of the NMAI, makes of the museum what West calls "a safe place for unsafe ideas": a place where "Native peoples can interpret their cultural inheritance and contemporary lives."

The bringing of a living Native cultural inheritance into the contemporary moment is a key survivance move. Emil Her Many Horses describes, from his perspective as a permanent curator at the NMAI, the practical challenges and efforts to develop the inaugural exhibitions, singling out "the section *Our Universes*, [where] we stressed native philosophies, Indigenous cosmologies, traditional ways of explaining the creation and order of the universe." This emphasis on Native epistemology and worldview is described also by Sven Haakanson, director of the Alutiiq Museum in Kodiak, Alaska, who explains, "I know how important it is to make things, to transmit knowledge through the actual objects, through gestures, through active participation, through the sharing of knowledge by getting each person to create a piece. This experience links them to our history in ways only creating can—one on one and hands on."

For Richard West, this survivance hermeneutic works through the objects of the NMAI collection; elsewhere, Gerald Vizenor describes this same epistemology operating through a lexicon of "shadow words" that elude and exceed the conceptual reach of European discourses. This vocabulary of survivance endures as the "tragic wisdom" that the tribes have achieved through the difficult history of European contact, one of the many traces of tribal presence that Vizenor describes as "the remanence of intransitive shadows."[3] An intransitive verb has no object; an intransitive shadow has no object but is only itself. Literally, "remanence" signifies the magnetic force that remains within an object once the external magnetizing field has been removed. This is a powerful metaphor for an understanding of Native identity that is not a shadow of something from the past, something that came before, but is its own self and remains its own integral self despite the comings and goings of external forces. Native tribal identity sustains itself independently of European influences. More than this, however, the metaphor suggests that European discourses, in the presence of Native cultures, acquire Native elements that remain as remanences even after Native communities have been removed to the margins of the dominant society. Though Native American writers, journalists, lawyers, politicians, and artists may use the English language, the language that they use is infused with the survivance of Native tribal cultures. Words like "remanence" can, within a survivance hermeneutic, signify meanings that cast metaphorical lexical shadows across accustomed meanings and stories that support dominant forms of nation-state sovereignty.

Survivance is a Native form of telling history. For example, for nearly a decade Vizenor campaigned for the University of California at Berkeley to recognize the service provided to the university by the last Yahi man, Ishi. In 1992, Vizenor wrote to the chancellor that "the very institutions and the foundational wealth of this state are based on stolen land and the murder of tribal people."[4] Finally, in 1993, the central courtyard of Dwinelle Hall was named Ishi Court. At the dedication ceremony, Vizenor angrily declared: "There is a wretched silence in the histories of this state and nation: the silence of tribal names. The landscapes are burdened with untrue discoveries. There are no honorable shadows in the names of dominance. The shadows of tribal names and stories persist, and the shadows are our natural survivance."[5] Again, Vizenor uses the image of shadows to suggest the suppressed histories that endure in words and especially in names. In the names that the state buildings do in fact bear is the disavowed colonial history of theft and murder; the unspoken shadow meanings of these names are not "honorable." However, in the name Ishi Court is to be found the remanence of Native presence and a reminder of the enduring Native possession of place.

The limited understanding of history supported by the names assigned to places and buildings by the state is symptomatic of the limitations of European epistemologies acknowledged within a survivance worldview. It is the understanding of the limits of settler knowledge that provides the basis for survivance in its original French meaning. *Survivance* signifies the qualification to inherit an estate and formal recognition of the legal status of a survivor. Or, in Vizenor's words to Joëlle Rostkowski, "[s]urvivance . . . is the heritable right of succession or reversion of an estate, and, in the course of international declarations of human rights, a narrative estate of native survivance." What this means in a Native context is the readiness of individuals and communities alike to continue the transmission of tribal cultures, values, and knowledge to future generations, through international and domestic legal instruments, through creative storying in literature, art, music, and through the practices of everyday life.

Sven Haakanson relates how his grandmother spoke to him in the Alutiiq language that was denied his parents; N. Scott Momaday talks here about the personal confidence and communal traditions he inherited from his parents. Momaday speaks also of his personal commitment to the passing on of this inheritance, in part through the establishment of the Buffalo Trust, the objective of which he describes as "to revive traditional culture, to reinforce the dialogue between generations." He continues, "I want to foster the development of local archives where oral tradition can be preserved, Native stories videotaped and where young people could have access to computers, where they could listen to old tales told by elders and, in a very casual way, rediscover their roots." Momaday's strategy of bringing the past into the present by imagining oral stories told via computer is a survivance strategy of preserving the past not in some nostalgic and static history but in the modern present. Survivance here is much more than survival or physical endurance; survivance is a Native way of knowing that signifies a sustaining, living, tribal presence now and in the future.

The epistemological claim for the power of survivance is intrinsically connected to a creative, transformative ontological practice. Survivance is not only a way of interpreting through resistance—that resistance itself creates the world it brings into being through counternarratives. Like the "earthdivers" of Anishinaabe storying, those who see the world in terms of survivance recreate that world anew. But this renewed world is that of enduring tribal presence, the tribal estate inherited and instantiated through survivance. The often baroque, often satirical works by Anishinaabe artist David Bradley exemplify this act of counterstorying. The narrative paintings that express Bradley's ironic vision see the world in terms of a Native ontology. His Native reappropriation of iconic historical moments inverts the priorities that structure a colonialist vision of reality. Bradley's 1982 painting *How the West Was Lost*, for example, reverses the terms of the phrase "How the West Was Won." The subversive power of Bradley's work arises from his ability to put into conversation opposing notions of the real and to give priority to the Native. As he tells Joëlle Rostkowski, "I perceive myself both as an artist and as an Indian Rights activist inviting collectors and art lovers to reconsider history and contemporary society."

A foundational aspect of survivance ontology is the refusal to accept Western linear time or calendar time over tribal understandings of time. Suzan Harjo responds to the question concerning the important events that shaped her life by recalling her ancestors and events that happened before her lifetime, like the Sand Creek Massacre and the Battles of Little Bighorn and Palo Duro Canyon. She explains, "In the Cheyenne language, we have no past tense. Only Is and Is Coming. It means that what happened in the past is still present in your consciousness and in your life. The Muscogee have known the Battle of Horseshoe Bend and the Trail of Tears. These still are on our minds. Things that happened before my lifetime actually are happening to me." The present reality of what in European terms is represented as the past constitutes a fundamental distinction between Western and Native ontologies.

The articulation of a tribal ontology within the context of survivance necessarily involves the representation of transformation, whether between Western and tribal understandings of the nature of time, or the interchangeable transformations of the human into animal and animal into human, or the transformation of the nature of place through Native geographical movement. Vizenor's concept of "transmotion" names these survivance practices of transformation. Native transmotion is a practice of ontological transformation that overcomes the separations imposed by a colonial ontology or worldview. More than this, Native movement is an assertion of presence that is neither granted nor controlled by the state; as Vizenor asserts, "Motion is a natural human right that is not bound by borders." Tribal movement, then, is an assertion of political sovereignty independent of the provisions of colonialist treaties. Treaties regulate sovereignty over land but not over people, so transmotion is a survivance strategy and assertion of this Native sovereignty of the people.

Travel, both within the United States and internationally, marks the careers of many of the people interviewed here. David Bradley tells how his travels with the Peace Corps in Guatemala, Haiti, and Costa Rica, along with his interest in Eastern European and Asian painting, broadened the experience that informs his art. Tony Abeyta explains how his formation as an artist developed through his movement from Santa Fe to Baltimore, then to New York and Chicago, and was further inspired by his travels in Europe, particularly France and Italy. He explains, "I create from a Native American vocabulary but I am inspired by the knowledge I have acquired from other parts of the world, and from various periods of art history." For Native artists like Bradley and Abeyta, cosmopolitan experience facilitates a Native transformation of the Western artistic heritage, revising the nature of the reality created through those works of art. The creation of transformative art is a survivance practice.

Vizenor's concept of "fugitive poses" describes another form of survivance as an axiology, a mode of being or state of analytical consciousness. His book *Fugitive Poses* is subtitled *Native American Indian Scenes of Absence and Presence*, evoking the terms of the dynamic relationship between absence and presence, colonialism and tribalism, dominance and survivance that shape the possibilities for Native identities. The absence of real Native people from nation-state histories creates a double absence when real Natives are represented instead by the invented figure of the "Indian." While the destructive cultural effect of Native stereotypes is indisputable, Vizenor draws attention to tribal people who have created out of these impossible stereotypes of Indians who never existed new possibilities for living on their own terms. The simulated Indian offers material from which to construct a discursive defense or shield, under cover of which survivance identities can flourish. In his autobiography, *Interior Landscapes*, Vizenor writes of his grandmother Alice Beaulieu who practiced survivance under cover of "fugitive poses." He tells how she and her much younger, blind husband would travel by bus into the Minneapolis suburbs and, selling brushes door-to-door, would engage lonely housewives in creative and life-sustaining storytelling.

Louisita Warren in her interview tells Joëlle Rostkowski how some members of her pueblo coped with the imposition of Catholicism by adopting a "fugitive pose":

"some of us became very devout Christians, without necessarily giving up their traditional religion. But, for many others, conversion has been merely a screen, an acceptance hiding real beliefs. . . . My uncle used to tell me that Christianity was like a coat that we could wear to hide our traditional clothes."

The emphasis upon everyday practices represents survivance as an axiology with profound epistemological and ontological capacities to bring into a condition of presence the enduring Indigeneity of Native America. Taking the heritage of tribal resistance and endurance into the modern world is a survivance axiology. This resistance involves challenging the demeaning racialist imagery of Indian stereotypes promoted, for example, through sports mascots and conservative museum policies. Jill Momaday explains that she left the acting profession after she realized that, "being a Native girl, I would be confined inevitably to a representation of some stereotypical image or role: Indian princess or hooker. The interesting parts were not there." Veronica Tiller, a Native American historian, explains in her interview that "The historical perception of Native Americans, all the stereotypical images conveyed by history books, has had a major impact on the way we have been perceived by other Americans. We are still seen as a dependent people and I wanted to say that there is another perspective. We, as Native Americans, must write our own history and stories. We must get the message out through all forms of media, through books, through documentation on the Internet, cable TV, films, workshops and at meetings." Mohawk educator, journalist, and United Nations representative Kenneth Deer's work had advanced this survivance practice not only through First Nations Native education but also through his creation of the newspaper *The Eastern Door*. He explains that he established this Native newspaper "because there was no information in mainstream media on Kahnawake or on matter of interest to us. Most information in the mainstream was generally sensationalist and inaccurate."

In addition to the effort to reclaim the full range of possibilities for Native identity, survivance practices also include important work to reclaim tribal lands, to revitalize Native languages, to defend historic treaty rights, to obtain legal protection for sacred places, to support tribal sovereignty in gaming legislation, and to achieve improvements in education and healthcare. Erma Vizenor's account of her courageous struggle against corruption within tribal governance, and her election as the first woman to lead the White Earth Nation, demonstrates that the resistance foundational to survivance must be practiced in both tribal and non-Native contexts.

In this way, survivance is not a return to the past in the manner of nostalgia or misplaced romanticism; rather, survivance is a mode of being and acting in the world that continually seeks to reconcile living tribal values with the reality of modernity. But this process of reconciliation is grounded in the critical consciousness of tribal ontology and epistemology. Reconciliation in the context of survivance is the opposite of assimilation, where change occurs on the colonizer's rather than tribal terms. Métis dancer and choreographer Rulan Tangen explains how the mission of her company, Dancing Earth, Indigenous Contemporary Dance Creations, is to create hybrid performances with "interwoven philosophies, mixing various Indigenous cultures." This is not a pan-Indian effort; rather, she describes how "Our message tends to be intertribal. The dancers would be recognizable through their hairstyle, whether it is Mohawk, Apache, or Lakota. We would be mixing elements from three or four tribes and weave them all together in a performance that would express our common concerns, our determination to cling to our roots, to remain faithful to our cultures."

The legal instruments created in response to Native activism represent another important aspect of the work of survivance to inscribe the Native presence that is integral to contemporary society. Among the extraordinary people interviewed in this book are those activists whose work resulted in legislation such as the National Historic Preservation Act (1966, amended 2006), the American Indian Religious Freedom Act (1978), the Native American Graves Protection and Repatriation Act (1990), the Indian Arts and Crafts Act (1990), and the United Nations Declaration on the Rights of Indigenous Peoples (2007).

The founder and executive director of the Indian Law Resource Center, Tim Coulter, tells the story of his role in the formulation of the UN Declaration, starting with his part in the drafting of a Declaration of Principles, submitted at a major 1977 conference hosted by the United Nations in Geneva concerned with discrimination against the Indigenous peoples of the Americas. He continues his story through the granting of NGO status to the Indian Law Resource Center, the establishment of the UN Working Group on Indigenous Populations and the Permanent Forum on Indigenous Issues, and his work on the UN Declaration. Coulter's story is in conversation here with Kenneth Deer's narrative of his involvement with the UN, especially during the Oka crisis of 1990, and his work as coordinator of the Indigenous Caucus of both the Working Group on Indigenous Populations and the Working Group on the Draft Declaration on the Rights of Indigenous Peoples.

Survivance insists that the image of the "Indian" evoked in colonialist discourses is a dangerous and damaging construction of the European imagination. The "Native" is real and present in the context of tribal heritage expressed through endurance, survival, resistance, and the readiness to inherit and pass on this Native tribal presence. Survivance is Native sovereignty; in the conversations that follow, Joëlle Rostkowski encourages her interviewees to explore their experience of survivance through the diverse aesthetic, cultural, and political contexts in which they have lived. The stories told by these remarkable people underline the changes wrought in the conditions of Native America in the course of the twentieth century and into the twenty-first. That these changes are the result of intense commitment and struggle emerges from the personal stories we are privileged to hear. But these stories are always also communal stories based on the tribal inheritances that have been preserved and passed down through the generations. These are survivance stories informed by what Gerald Vizenor calls "tragic wisdom": the knowledge gleaned by tribal communities after centuries of dealing with colonialist nation-state governments.

Tim Coulter's assessment of the current state of Indigenous rights is sobering: he describes how "Indian people are no longer hunted down and shot in South America. Massacres are now relatively infrequent. I am grateful for that, truly. Many countries now accord self-determination to Indigenous peoples and respect (more or less) their land and resource rights. Indigenous peoples now have a permanent right to exist as peoples. These are historic advances in our civilization. Here, in the United States, very little has improved, and much has grown worse. Until recently I considered that Obama had done nothing of significance but I continued to be hopeful and I was extremely pleased when the President announced, on 16 December, 2010, the endorsement of the UN Declaration on the Rights of Indigenous Peoples. The Declaration sets an agenda for the United States and Indian nations to design a reasonable approach to a progressive realization of the duties and responsibilities in it; we should use the UN Declaration as a powerful affirmation of our rights. The rights proclaimed in the Declaration can be used to support and advocate for positive legislation and positive government action. What is important is that now we have a worldwide consensus on the Declaration—no country opposes it. This means a great deal for its future implementation. It also means that the United States as well as other countries will expect one another to respect the rights in the Declaration. This will add to the respect that countries give to indigenous rights in practice.

From forgotten Americans to Indigenous rights

Joëlle Rostkowski

Few have been more marginalized and ignored by Washington for as long as Native Americans, our First Americans.
    —Barack Obama, White House Tribal Nations Conference, November 5, 2009

Be the change you want to see in the world.
    —Mahatma Gandhi, as told to his grandson,
in "Arun Gandhi Shares the Mahatma's Message," by Michael W. Potts

Let us speak, not of the death of dreams but of the sustenance of dreams.
    —N. Scott Momaday, UNESCO nomination as Artist of Peace, May 12, 2004

This collection of sixteen conversations illustrates some of the major developments that have marked Native American life during the last thirty years. Agents of change, actors of history, the persons interviewed in this volume have—in one way or another—witnessed major social upheavals. Most of them have, directly and indirectly, been instrumental in cultural revitalization and achieved important goals in the literary, artistic, legal, or political fields. They have engaged in individual and collective struggles to remain faithful to their roots while opening up to new challenges. They have overcome personal trauma or discrimination through their own creativity, endurance, and fortitude. They have, personally and professionally, encouraged the assertion of Native identity but also interacted actively with mainstream America. Several of them have been ambassadors of Native cultures on the international scene. Through their own words the contributors explain in the following conversations how they have tried to remain faithful to their childhood dreams, have engaged in struggles to confer more visibility to Indian issues, and have played a role in Native American resistance and renaissance.

This book is about the remarkable men and women that I have met through my research on American Indian history. It is based upon extraordinary encounters, working relationships established and reinforced over the years, common endeavors and experiences shared. It deals with the search for wisdom, the power to overcome obstacles, the capacity to shape one's destiny.

BEING AN OUTSIDER

The twenty-first century was almost ten years old. The year was coming to an end. President Obama addressed Native American leaders on Thursday, November 5,

2009 to acknowledge the "Nation's troubled relationships" and to pledge to redeem broken promises.

It was the first White House meeting of its kind since 1994. More than four hundred tribes were represented. As he was stressing his determination to reverse the federal government's history of neglecting the plight of Indian nations, the president was expressing his empathy, because of his own history as "an outsider."

I understand what it means to be an outsider. . . . I was born to a teenage mother. My father left when I was two years old, leaving her—my mother and my grandparents to raise me . . . I understand what it means to be on the outside looking in. I know what it means to feel ignored and forgotten.[1]

Coming from Barack Obama, whose father was Kenyan and who is the first African American president of the United States, this message implied an acknowledgment of past distress and recognition of the importance of social and cultural diversity. It expressed personal concern for discrimination and the belief, reinforced by an exceptional destiny, in the capacity of the human spirit to overcome obstacles and to make every effort to improve the course of history.

PROMISES TO KEEP

Barack Obama's speech was phrased in very general terms: the president promised to give American Indians a better voice in his administration and signed an executive order requiring the Cabinet members to consult regularly and efficiently with Indian tribes. It was mentioned that a similar order issued by President Clinton had not been implemented efficiently by some agencies: "over the last nine years, only a few agencies have made an effort to implement that executive order—and it's time for a change."

President Obama told Indian leaders that his administration was deeply concerned, at the close of 2009, with the failing economy and didn't forget the specific problems of Indian communities such as unemployment and high poverty rates. He reminded them that his administration had allocated more than $3 billion in stimulus for tribal communities, much of it for school improvement and $500 million for strengthening and modernizing the Indian Health Service (IHS). In his speech, the president recognized that Native Americans were still facing dramatic problems:

Some of your reservations face unemployment rates of up to 80 percent. Roughly a quarter of all Native Americans live in poverty. More than 14 percent of all reservation homes don't have electricity; and 12 percent don't have access to a safe water supply. In some reservations, as many as 20 people live together just to get by. Without real communication and consultation, we're stuck year after year with policies that don't work on issues specific to you and on broader issues that affect all of us. And you deserve to have a voice in both.

Spurring job creation; improving the IHS in order to fight high rates of tuberculosis, alcoholism, diabetes, pneumonia, and influenza; fighting educational problems such as low matriculation, high school and college drop-out rates; and developing clean energy on Indian land were among the priorities defined by President Obama.

FROM "THE FORGOTTEN AMERICAN" TO INDIGENOUS RIGHTS

On March 6, 1968, in his special message to Congress entitled "The Forgotten American," President Lyndon Johnson declared: "For two centuries [the American Indian] has been an alien in his own land." Johnson then proposed "a new goal for Indian programs . . . a goal that . . . ends termination and stresses self-determination." He was setting in motion the concept of self-determination and leading federal Indian policy away from the assimilation-based Termination policy that had marked the 1950s. Indians were included in much of the president's Great Society legislation, continuing a trend begun during the previous administration. By executive order Johnson established the National Council on Indian Opportunity, chaired by the vice president, Hubert Humphrey, to coordinate the various agencies dealing with Indian matters and to promote their involvement in the planning of Indian programs.

As Vine Deloria Jr., brilliant essayist and policy advocate, has pointed out, the gap between "high-level pronouncements" and the "nebulous arena of implementation" is often source of disappointment.[2] The end of the 1960s was characterized by demonstrations and major social and political confrontations. The history of American Indian activism started as a reaction against the Termination era. Implemented in only a few instances, Termination had disastrous consequences. And, for many years, the threat of its enforcement still hung over Indian communities. As the move toward self-determination gained momentum at the federal level, Indians began uniting to take control of their own future.

In the 1960s and 1970s, with ups and downs, encouraged by the Civil Rights movement, and under the new slogan of "Red Power," Native Americans, together with African Americans, Hispanic Americans, American youth, and women, challenged discrimination. Indian activism's persistence was remarkable and, actually, some of the most intense Indian protest occurred in the 1970s "when the civil rights movement was waning."[3]

The Red Power movement insisted on asserting its specificity, putting in evidence the fact that the First Americans, as a territorial minority, because of their link with the land, their history of dispossession marked by tragedy and deculturation, deserved special attention and recognition. Indian activism expressed a growing sense of pan-Indian identity and encompassed many intertribal organizations and various political tendencies. Challenging the moderate views of the National Congress of American Indians (NCAI) created in 1944, the National Indian Youth Council (NIYC), founded in 1961, became the voice of a new generation of leaders, eager to demand equal opportunity policies and better access to healthcare, education, employment, and leadership in government and economic development. The American Indian Movement (AIM) founded in 1968 by Dennis Banks and Russell Means became the most radical Native American activist group.

INVISIBLE, VISIBLE, INDIVISIBLE . . .

I am an invisible man. . . . I am invisible . . . simply because people refuse to see me . . . it is as though I have been surrounded by mirrors of hard, distorting glass. When they approach me they see only my surroundings, themselves, or figments of their imagination—indeed, everything and anything except me.
—Ralph Ellison, *The Invisible Man*

Some spectacular happenings conferred more visibility to Native Americans, challenging the old stereotypes. The occupation of Alcatraz Island and its derelict federal prison for nineteen months by "Indians of all Tribes" in San Francisco Bay drew attention to the need for political but also cultural recognition. In a wry comment, the occupants compared Alcatraz to an Indian reservation, because of its lack of resources, infrastructure, and its barren soil. They also asked for the establishment of a cultural and educational center in San Francisco Bay. Although they did not accomplish that goal, they managed to obtain nationwide news coverage. By the end of the siege, however, the *San Francisco Chronicle* reported scenes of ruin and mindless destruction and conveyed a very negative image of the occupiers.

The Bureau of Indian Affairs (BIA) takeover lasted only six days in November 1972. Some five hundred Indians, protesting against the government policies, presented a twenty-point program including the reestablishment of treaty relations between the federal government and Indian nations. Although it failed to have a real impact, it put in evidence some questionable practices concerning the management of Indian land and mineral resources. A few months later the occupation of Wounded Knee on the Pine Ridge Lakota reservation, by armed militants led by AIM leaders, to denounce the corruption of the BIA and of Richard Wilson's elected tribal government, drew worldwide media coverage. As in the case of the Alcatraz takeover, the press was initially sympathetic, even if the complex situation of the Pine Ridge reservation was not at the center of most people's concerns.

Wounded Knee, scene of the 1890 massacre when some three hundred unarmed Minneconjou Indians fleeing from one reservation to another were fired upon by Seventh Cavalry soldiers, was a dramatic historical and geographical landmark. The Wounded Knee massacre marked the end of the frontier. "From Wounded Knee to Wounded Knee" became a powerful slogan in 1973 and an interesting topic of historical research. It inspired many editorials. Moreover, in 1973, the name Wounded Knee was in the minds of all readers of Dee Brown's bestseller published a couple of years earlier: *Bury My Heart at Wounded Knee*, a powerful, well documented, and successful chronicle of the Indian wars. In the following pages Suzan Harjo makes reference to the importance of communication with the media during the Wounded Knee takeover and more specifically to the role of her husband, Frank Ray Harjo, who reported on the WBAI-FM radio station. WBAI, a noncommercial listener-supported radio station broadcasting in New York City, played a historic role in the support and development of the counterculture in the 1960s and 1970s.

The defense of Indian rights—on reservations and in urban areas—and the struggle against discrimination became priorities and were institutionalized. The late 1960s and 1970s saw the establishment of several legal service programs and organizations such as the American Indian Law Center (1967) at the University of New Mexico, Albuquerque; the Native American Rights Fund (1970) in Boulder, Colorado; and the Indian Law Resource Center (1978) in Washington, D.C. An increased number of Indians had access to legal programs in major universities and in the recently established Native colleges.

A new generation of journalists also conferred more visibility to Indian matters. The history of Indian newspapers goes back a long way, with the *Cherokee Phoenix*, the first tribal paper, created in 1828, and other important tribal papers such as *The Progress*, the first newspaper published more than a century ago on the White Earth Chippewa Reservation, Minnesota. But the development of national newspapers such as the *Akwesasne News* (1969) in the wake of the Red Power movement and, later on, *Indian Country Today* and *News from Indian Country*, changed the course of Indian policy during the 1970s and 1980s.

Eloquent policy advocates participated in the development of the Native press. Suzan Harjo was among them, and Kenneth Deer was the founder of *The Eastern Door*, a weekly paper serving the Mohawk community. As for Gerald Vizenor, he started his writing career as a journalist with the *Minneapolis Tribune*. Native papers were part of Indian activism. They established channels of communication between various communities and stimulated debates on the national scene, for example, in the museum field, during the complex discussions that took place in the 1980s within the Smithsonian Institution before the opening of the National Museum of the American Indian (NMAI). Some remarkable articles published in Native papers, in particular articles by columnist Suzan Harjo in *Indian Country Today*, document the active lobbying that went on behind the scenes and contributed greatly to the genesis of the NMAI, before it was established by an act of Congress in 1989.

The Native American Journalists' Association (NAJA) was created in 1984. In the midsummer of 2009, NAJA celebrated its twenty-fifth birthday in Albuquerque, New Mexico. Founders, including Tim Giago, who, in the late 1970s, started the *Lakota Times* (later to become *Indian Country Today*) with a few volunteers on the Pine Ridge Lakota Reservation, gathered to look back at the unity and diversity of Native journalism and its current perspectives. During the last decades, Native papers have expressed a multiplicity of Indian voices and concerns. Their archives now constitute historical documents.

As Kenneth Lincoln demonstrated in his book,[4] the last forty years were also marked by the beginning of an Indian renaissance in literature. One of the most prolific and provocative authors was Vine Deloria Jr., whose essay entitled *Custer Died for Your Sins*, published in 1969, became a bestseller and favored a reconsideration of Native history by mainstream America. It's also in 1969 that N. Scott Momaday received the Pulitzer Prize for his novel *House Made of Dawn*, paving the way for a new interest in Native writers by major national and international publishers. In chapter 1, Momaday looks back at his career as a poet, novelist, and painter. He discusses recent and lesser-known endeavors such as his travels to Siberia, his interest in visual arts, and his recognition on the international scene as a UNESCO Artist for Peace. Alan Velie, in his book entitled *Four Native American Literary Masters: A Study of James Welch, Scott Momaday, Gerald Vizenor, and Leslie Silko*[5] published in 1982 also put "Native American literature and Native American authors on the American cultural map."[6]

Since the early 1980s, Native American literature has flourished, as have Native American studies in many universities in North America and in Europe. Committed publishers, all over Europe, and particularly in Italy, France, and Germany, have published translations of novels by N. Scott Momaday, James Welch, Leslie Silko, Gerald Vizenor, Louis Owens, Louise Erdrich, and Sherman Alexie.

Vizenor and Momaday look back on this publishing explosion and on their own literary choices, affinities, and accomplishments. They both discuss their determination to contribute to the political and cultural advancement of their communities, through several commitments and endeavors: Vizenor has been instrumental in the drafting and adoption of a new constitution on White Earth Reservation and Momaday has created the Buffalo Trust, whose objective is to revive traditional culture and favor the transmission of knowledge among the Kiowa of Rainy Mountain in Oklahoma.

As Suzan Harjo points out in chapter 2, many radical ideas and writings have been signed into law in the past decades: "We achieved the American Indian Religious Freedom Act (1978), the National Museum of the American Indian (1989), the Native American Graves Protection and Repatriation Act (1990), and other laws to revitalize Native languages and return lands." Although there were sharp differences of opinion between various Native American organizations, they all contributed to major changes of perspective in mainstream America. In the museum field, for example, major reforms have taken place. One of the most spectacular changes occurred when it was decided that the National Museum of the American Indian would be built in Washington, D.C. and become home to the collection of the former Museum of the American Indian, Heye Foundation (New York) including more than 800,000 objects. The collection, assembled by George Gustav Heye (1874–1957) became part of the Smithsonian in June 1990. Harjo stresses the important role of some members of the Native intelligentsia such as Deloria and Momaday. With them and with the help of a committed group of supporters and influential policy advocates, she contributed actively to the reappropriation of Native heritage and to the opening, in Washington, D.C. of a brand new museum mostly run by American Indians.

When the National Museum of the American Indian (NMAI) opened its doors on September 21, 2004, its design, its philosophy, and its specificity remained very controversial. Its opening was a tremendous success as thousands of American Indians gathered and marched on the Mall in full regalia and met with friendly American and foreign tourists who had never visited Native communities and were not familiar with their history. But some editorials were critical, in particular a publicized and often quoted article written by Edward Rothstein in the *New York Times* entitled "Museum with an American Indian Voice" (September 21, 2004), in which the author sharply deplored the lack of scholarship and what he considered as "self-celebratory romance."

The elegance of the original building design, by Blackfoot architect Douglas Cardinal, with its soft curving walls in Kasota limestone, its surrounding garden planted with traditional Native crops, its large open atrium and, above all, its three permanent exhibitions (*Our Universes, Our Peoples: Giving Voices to Our Histories*, and *Our Lives: Contemporary Life and Identities*) were perceived as revolutionary. The NMAI was criticized as an identity museum, celebrating the survival of Native American cultures instead of providing scholarly anthropological documentation on the Heye collection. The exhibition on *Native Modernism*—curated by Truman Lowe and presenting the works of two of the most remarkable Native artists of the twentieth century, George Morrison (Chippewa, 1919–2000) and Allan Houser (Apache, 1914–1994)—was a great popular success, but remained controversial because some considered that it would have been more appropriate in an art museum.

In chapter 3 Richard West, founding director of the NMAI, explains the philosophy of what was conceived as a "museum different," a civic space celebrating the survival of Native peoples, but also favoring intercultural dialogue. He stresses what has inspired his leadership and what he would like to consider as his legacy: the encounter with living cultures, the respect for the sacredness and power of objects, the confrontation not only with Native artifacts but also with Native experience. As the son of a gifted Native artist he also reaffirms the importance of devoting some space to contemporary Native art.

Emil Her Many Horses, curator at the National Museum of the American Indian, evokes his past experience as director of the small tribal Rosebud Museum (Rosebud Lakota Reservation, South Dakota), and his fruitful contribution to some of the most successful exhibitions put together by the NMAI: the permanent exhibition *Our Universes* and the temporary exhibits entitled *Identity by Design* and *Song for a Horse Nation*. As a Lakota Native of South Dakota, who received an education with an emphasis on philosophy and religion, he has proved committed to putting in evidence the spiritual dimension of Native cultures. He also has documented the important role of women in the preservation of Native heritage.

Sven Haakanson, director of the Alutiiq Museum in Kodiak, Alaska, shares with us in chapter 5 his extraordinary destiny as a young Sugpiag brought up in Alaska, where the memory of Russian rule and Orthodox religion are still quite vivid (he still remembers learning by heart all the Orthodox prayers in Old Church Slavonic). He has been instrumental in the cultural revival of his community and has initiated an exceptionally successful experience of intercultural dialogue with the French Musée-Château of Boulogne-sur-Mer, paving the way for further mediation between cultural institutions and museums at the international level.

PAST IS PRESENT

> The past is never dead. It's not even past.
> —William Faulkner

"In the Cheyenne language, we have no past tense," says Suzan Harjo, "only Is and Is Coming. It means that what has happened in the past is still present in your consciousness and in your life. . . . "Things that happened before my lifetime actually are happening to me."

The presence of history and the memory of past suffering in individual and collective life is implicitly present in each interview, as is the determination to overcome trauma and assert one's identity. "My parents, grandparents and great-grandparents were beaten up in federal boarding schools for speaking their heritage languages," says Suzan Harjo, "but they managed to keep them and pass them on . . . my father used to run away from school and he was often chased by the bounty hunters who were paid five dollars for each runaway child. My mother was horribly abused but wouldn't talk about it." And she adds that her parents taught her how to relate to the past, told her the truth but did not overburden her with the tragedy of their history. "A people is not defeated until the hearts of its women are on the ground." This Cheyenne saying, quoted by Harjo, is illustrated by the inner strength and the endurance of all the women interviewed in this book.

Erma Vizenor, tribal chairwoman of the White Earth Reservation and the subject of the interview in chapter 7, is another example of determination and fortitude. She has engaged in fights against corrupt leaders and had to face those who were not ready to accept a woman in a leadership position: "My days, months and years as a tribal leader are far from easy. Not everyone likes me. A few do not like a woman chief. I am a visionary, progressive leader, which infuriates those who do not want change. . . . I have seen the fear and intimidation of dictator leaders and their patronage."

Louisita Warren, elder of Santa Clara pueblo (New Mexico), mother of Dave Warren—historian, consultant, and one of the former presidents of the Institute of American Indian Arts (IAIA)—shares with us in chapter 8 some memories of her life in her pueblo, at the beginning of the twentieth century. She reflects on the complex sociopolitical and religious frameworks of "compartmentalization" in the pueblos of New Mexico, with two socio-ceremonial systems, the Indigenous system and the Christian system established by the Franciscan missionaries. In spite of bitter childhood memories of her confrontations with a narrow-minded missionary, and together with her strong conviction of being "a rebel," Louisita Warren pleads for understanding, forgiveness, and tolerance. She found serenity and a profound sense of accomplishment in her personal spiritual quest, the preservation of her traditional heritage, the accomplishments of her son, and her strong family values. At the end of the interview she declares: "if I were given the opportunity to live a second life and to select my identity, I would choose to be Indian once again. It has been a beautiful experience."

Veronica Tiller, the subject of the interview in chapter 6, is a remarkable example of a woman who embarked on several successful careers: as a historian, consultant, publisher of reference books, and manager of her own company, she has proved that traditions and modernity can be successfully combined. She never let discrimination discourage her: "We were considered as savages, as pagans, as late as the 1950s and early 1960s. . . . We, as Native Americans, must write our own history and stories. . . . Otherwise we'll continue to be victimized and stereotyped."

Jill Momaday and Rulan Tangen, the subjects of the interviews in chapters 12 and 13, respectively, have been actively involved in the assertion of their identity as Native women who want to reach out beyond traditional stereotypes. Both of them had the possibility to be recognized as modern incarnations of the "Indian princess," and yet they have refused to be used by the media to perpetuate old clichés. Age-old stereotypes have been difficult to eradicate. As many scholars have pointed out, Indian women have been portrayed—by anthropologists, historians, but also in films and in advertisement campaigns—from a Euro-American male perspective. This is what Momaday points out through her experience as a model and actress, because she rebelled against the stereotypical representation of Indian women in the film industry: "I knew very well that, being a Native girl, I would be confined inevitably to a representation of some stereotypical image or role: Indian princess or hooker." Both Momaday and Tangen have shown their determination to dispense with the Indian maiden or "supersquaw" stereotypes, while fending for themselves and conquering the role of modern ambassadors of Native cultures. Momaday has become the "face" of New Mexico, through her activities as Chief of Protocol, and Tangen, as a dancer and choreographer, has asserted her Métis identity through her Dancing Earth Indigenous Company, becoming a pioneer in the field of contemporary dance.

The development of contemporary Native art, over the last forty years, often characterized as "postmodernism," has also contributed to confer more visibility to Indian issues. In chapter 10 David Bradley (Anishinaabe) reinterprets art historical imagery and Native stereotypes with irony. Trained at the Institute of American Indian Arts (IAIA) in Santa Fe, Bradley deconstructs popular myths and offers his sarcastic vision of history and modernity. His work is striking and interesting from a historical point of view. In the following interview he says: "I perceive myself both as an artist and as an Indian activist inviting collectors and art lovers to reconsider history and contemporary society." Like many contemporary Native artists, Bradley is inspired by his Indian identity. He has been among those who were in favor of the Indian Arts and Crafts Act of November 29, 1990, adopted to protect the Native American art market from fraud.

Darren Vigil Gray (Jicarilla Apache), the subject of the interview in chapter 11, was like David Bradley trained at the IAIA and he also reinterprets history, but in a more internalized and sometimes abstract way, revisiting some Apache rituals like the mysterious and spectacular dancing of the crown dancers and projecting his own perception of space and time into his large frescoes of the Southwestern landscape or powerful portraits.

Traditional themes are also at the core of work of Tony Abeyta (Navajo), the subject of chapter 9. The artist's warm earthly colors and delicate paintings of fauna and flora, sometimes reinterpreted in an abstract manner, seem to emanate from the soil of New Mexico and communicate the warmth and vibrations of nature. His additional training in Europe and his familiarity with the Renaissance masters, Italian mosaics, and frescoes have added a singular finish to the intensity of his paintings and to his murals. He likes to say that he works from "a Native American vocabulary" but is inspired by the knowledge he has acquired from other parts of the world.

Over the last several decades Native Americans have been exposed to world conflicts, other systems of governments, and other artistic and literary traditions. Many of the testimonies gathered in this volume make reference to the importance of time spent abroad as soldiers, students, or aspiring diplomats. Gerald Vizenor served twice in the United States Army. He lied about his age and enlisted at fifteen in the Minnesota National Guard. During the Korean War his service was entirely in

Japan where he met native Ainu on Hokkaido and discovered their association with the bears. He also was impressed by minimalist haiku poetry. In this book he tells us that "the images of haiku are instant, an immediate poetic heartbeat, an image of a natural scene or ironic situation." Haiku poetry has inspired him ever since. His experiences in Japan provided him with "the confidence to seriously consider poetry and literature" and he was enchanted to realize that "the imagistic practices of haiku were similar to the native dream songs of the Anishinaabeg."

N. Scott Momaday also expresses his strong interest in the discovery of other cultures. He enjoys working with other Indigenous peoples all over the world, in Siberia, Alaska, as well as in his own Kiowa community. The time he spent in Russia was particularly important for him. He found "a lot of energy for writing and drawing when he was there," and it was when he was visiting the Soviet Union that, suddenly what his father—who was an artist—had taught him "came to the surface." That's when he decided to start a painting career.

THE DISCOURSE OF INDIGENEITY: AN INTERNATIONAL STRUGGLE

The strong feeling of solidarity that has developed between Indigenous peoples during the last decades has been encouraged and supported by intertribal organizations, nongovernmental organizations, and the United Nations. The long process of recognition of Indigenous rights on the international scene has been difficult and controversial because the issue was perceived as highly political by member states within the United Nations.

Founding father

The interest that American Indians have demonstrated toward international organizations goes back to the first contacts established in 1923 by Chief Deskaheh (Haudenosaunee) who came to the League of Nations (Geneva, Switzerland) with his *Red Man's Appeal for Justice*. When Deskaheh left Europe in 1924, after frustrating negotiations, he was ill, "his heart was broken," and he had realized that, although Indians refer to themselves as Peoples or Nations, they would be considered for many years as "ethnic groups" and "minorities" by international organizations. The international community had widely supported the right of self-determination for peoples in European colonies but, in the post-colonial era, member states opposed self-determination for peoples within the territory of the United States because of their concern for territorial integrity. It was not until the 1970s that the right to self-determination was reconsidered and that American Indians were finally defined as "Indigenous peoples" rather than "minorities." Deskaheh's memory has been preciously preserved in the archives of the League. It is briefly evoked in the epilogue of this volume because, in spite of the chief's failure to obtain the recognition of Iroquois sovereignty, he paved the way for further negotiations of Native organizations on the international scene.

On the road to international recognition

The process that eventually led to Indian representation at the United Nations remained very slow while contacts were established solely on a tribal basis. It was through intertribal cooperation and the recognition of Native groups as nongovernmental organizations (NGOs) with consultative status that Indian delegations found a voice at the United Nations. NGOs regularly attend relevant UN meetings to which they can participate orally and through the submission of written statements. They also organize NGO conferences and meetings hosted by organizations of the UN system.

In September 1977 the International NGO Conference on Discrimination Against Indigenous Populations in the Americas was organized in Geneva within the framework of the Decade for Action to Combat Racism and Racial Discrimination (1973–1982). The conference brought together Indigenous representatives from the American continent, some two hundred delegates and observers, and many nongovernmental organizations. The arrival of Indian representatives in traditional costume in Geneva was a momentous occasion, abundantly reported by the local media although the emphasis was placed on the "quaintness" of the delegations rather than on the debates themselves. The Haudenosaunee and the Hopi, like Deskaheh fifty years earlier, used their own passports, which were considered acceptable entry documents by Swiss immigration officers.

The International NGO Conference on Indigenous Peoples and the Land was organized in September 1981 as a follow-up to the 1977 conference. Whereas the previous conference had concentrated on the American continent, the 1981 meeting was to extend to Asia and Africa the geographical representation of Indigenous peoples on the international scene. The main objective of the conference, which was attended by some three hundred delegates, observers, and guests, was to highlight the special relationship of Indigenous peoples with their land and their natural, original right to live freely within their own territories. The report of the conference endorsed some important suggestions, such as the establishment of a working group and the involvement of Indigenous groups in an increasing number of UN agencies, such as UNESCO.

The establishment of a special working group on Indigenous populations, as a subsidiary organ of the Subcommission on the Promotion and Protection of Human Rights, was an institutional victory, although the group was located at the lowest level of the hierarchy of UN human rights bodies. The first meeting of the group in August 1982 was the culmination of unrelenting efforts of a whole team of UN officials devoted to the cause of some of the most forgotten communities of the world. The group's work was based upon José R. Martinez Cobo's comprehensive report entitled "Study of the Problem of Discrimination Against Indigenous Populations," which was a general survey of pertinent provisions in national and international legislation.

The working group had flexible rules and was open to all Indigenous communities and organizations, even those who didn't have NGO credentials. The openness of its sessions and the intensity and creativity of its debates singled it out in the UN system and made it progressively more acceptable by member state governments, as they cautiously followed the reconsideration of the relationship between Indigenous peoples and states. The group was entrusted with a twofold mission: the review of developments pertaining to the promotion and protection of human rights of Indigenous peoples and the drafting of new standards for this new category of "peoples" at the national and international level.

Indigenous involvement in the United Nations progressed initially at an astonishing pace, in spite of inner conflicts, several crises, and the lack of active cooperation of many suspicious governments who considered the Native groups present in Geneva as non-representative of established tribal governments. But Indigenous representatives were actively supported by the UN Secretariat, the local press, and the spontaneous support of many volunteers, including interpreters, scholars, human rights associations, and legal experts.

A remarkable movement of solidarity marked the negotiations held in Geneva, within the framework of the annual meetings of the working group. The doCIP (Indigenous Peoples' Center for Documentation, Research and Information), a Swiss quadrilingual nonprofit institution, was set up in 1978 to provide assistance and information to newcomers. Over the years it developed various modes of assistance to the delegations present in Geneva, including orientation sessions on human rights mechanisms, provided regular updates on UN meetings through its newsletter, and established an online documentation center. The UN Secretariat got used to the rituals preceding the annual sessions of the working group at the end of July: dances and songs, blessings and collective prayers by Native peoples from all over the world in full regalia.

With the active participation of Indigenous organizations, the working group prepared a draft of the United Nations Declaration on the Rights of Indigenous Peoples (1993). This draft was adopted by the Subcommission for the Protection and Promotion of Human Rights in 1994 and went through the UN hierarchy, the expectation being that it would eventually be proclaimed by the General Assembly of the United Nations. In 1995 the draft was submitted to the Commission on Human Rights, which established an open-ended intersession working group to examine the text adopted by the subcommission. This new working group was an additional structure—restricted to established NGOs and more technical than the former group—whose mandate was the minute discussion and final drafting of every article. Semantics were at the core of the legal debates that took place within the group. The negotiations between Indigenous peoples and states then became particularly protracted and intense, continuing for more than a decade, until the adoption of the final text by the UN General Assembly in September 2007.

Among the most debated issues of the draft declaration was Article 3 on self-determination. Looking back to that bone of contention, James Anaya, Apache lawyer and Special Rapporteur on the situation of human rights and fundamental freedoms, analyzed the various conflicting interpretations of that concept in the following terms:

> Article 3 of the Declaration and its affirmation of indigenous self-determination proved to be one of the most contentious of the Declaration's provisions during the negotiations preceding its adoption. Independent of the subjective meaning attached to the right or principle of self-determination by indigenous peoples themselves, a frequent tendency has been to understand self-determination as wedded to attributes of statehood, with "full" self-determination deemed to be in the attainment of independent statehood, or at least in the right to choose independent statehood. For obvious reasons, this tendency made explicit affirmation of indigenous self-determination the subject of lively debate . . .[7]

For Native American groups, the notion of "self-determination" was of utmost importance: "for indigenous and for other peoples who have been subjected to colonialism or to other forms of oppressive dominion, self-determination is the word that captures the essence of their aspirations to survive and to prosper with freedom and dignity."[8] However, fears concerning rampant Indigenous secessionism had to be taken into account. In the final version of the Declaration, the right to self-determination in Article 3 remains unchanged, but its significance is curtailed by an addition to Article 46 (1) stipulating that nothing in the Declaration may be "construed as authorizing or encouraging any action which would dismember or impair totally or in part the territorial integrity or political unity of any state."

The recognition of collective rights also proved difficult and made the last years of negotiations very difficult. Some states claimed that the recognition of collective rights could be potentially discriminatory if they could prevail over the human rights of individuals.

In its final version the Declaration remains a significant document breaking new ground in the field of international law. It recognizes the importance of cultural diversity and individual and collective human rights of Indigenous peoples. It supports Indigenous peoples' claims to autonomy, control over land, freedom of religion and religious practices, protection of the environment through veto of projects deemed undesirable and far-reaching claims for restitution or compensation. It was finally adopted on September 13, 2007 by a vote of 143 to 4 with 11 abstentions. The four negative votes were all by states with sizeable numbers of Indigenous peoples: Australia, Canada, New Zealand, and the United States.

Since then, all of the four countries that had voted "no" progressively initiated a process that led them to reconsider their position. On April 3, 2009, the Australian government, in the spirit of re-settling its relationship with indigenous Australians, asserted its determination to preserve their heritage, and formally endorsed the Declaration, followed by New Zealand, on April 20, 2010. However it was made clear by both countries that their support for the Declaration was not unconditional and that it was considered as an "aspirational" document.

The Canadian government had proved a strong supporter of United Nations mechanisms but had expressed concerns with the wording of some of the Declaration's provisions. On November 12, 2010, "to further reconcile and strengthen" its relationship with "Aboriginal peoples" and also carefully defining the Declaration as an "aspirational" document, it formally endorsed it. John Duncan, Minister of Indian Affairs and Northern Development acknowledged that it was an important text setting out a number of principles that should guide harmonious and cooperative relationships based on equality, partnership, good faith and mutual respect.[9]

In his speech at the White House Tribal Nations Conference on December 16, 2010, President Obama, after a long and comprehensive interagency review and extensive consultation with tribes, announced that the United States had changed its position and was lending its support to the Declaration. "The aspirations it affirms," he said, "including the respect for the institutions and rich cultures of Native peoples, are one we must always seek to fulfill."[10] Shortly afterwards it was announced that U.S. agencies were engaged in numerous initiatives to address the concerns raised by Native American leaders and issues addressed in the Declaration.[11]

The United States was the last of the four countries that had previously voted against the Declaration to reverse its position. This endorsement was considered a victory and welcomed by most Indigenous lawyers and representatives as a long-overdue step forward. As Special Rapporteur on the Rights of Indigenous Peoples, James Anaya declared that it was a groundbreaking development in the field of human rights, adding that "the Declaration affirms the right of Indigenous peoples to continue their existence as distinct communities under conditions of equality within their traditional territories, and to retain and transmit to future generations their cultural identities."[12]

It was reported in *Indian Country Today* that some native leaders had expressed disappointment with the limitations the United States placed on its support, in particular the statement that the United States plans to recognize a new and distinct international concept of self-determination specific to indigenous peoples, different from the existing right of self-determination in international law.[13]

Robert T. Coulter, Director of the Indian Law Resource Center, pointed out that the endorsement of the Declaration marks the culmination of over three decades of very hard work by indigenous peoples and other members of the international human rights community.[14] In the following pages, he explains that this formal endorsement should be considered as a very positive move because it sets a new agenda for U.S.-Indian relations. According to him, the Declaration will be very useful to support and advocate for positive legislation and positive government action.

The Declaration has profoundly transformed the perspective on Indigenous issues, even in states who have voted against it. Until the 1980s it was held that the situation of Indigenous peoples was solely the concern of states, but the discourse of Indigeneity and the creation of a comprehensive body of standards concerning the way countries should treat Indigenous peoples had a normative impact on national policies and practices and on the evolution of Native rights. Universities have included courses on Indigenous rights, some research units deal specifically with the study and analysis of UN structures and instruments, journalists follow new developments on Indigenous issues, and a new generation of film directors has proved inspired by the defense of Indigenous environmental and spiritual values. This is why the Declaration can be considered as an important historical document, even if it is—inevitably—a compromise. It is a nonbinding instrument but provides an ethical framework for further reforms.

Looking back to the overall process that led to the recognition and formulation of Indigenous rights, it seems that, rather than focusing on arguments over the final wording of the Declaration, it is the progress accomplished in the field of Indian rights, the increased awareness encouraged by UN debates that has marked the last forty years. A change of perspective has taken place in the field of Indian law. New legal concepts have been forged or developed in many countries in the wake of those debates. They have already been used in court by informed lawyers, they have inspired new bills and they have been instrumental in the formulation of new projects. Indigenous peoples were latecomers in the process of the development of international law, but they have proved that they can play an active and pivotal role in the defense of their own rights.

STORIES AND HISTORY

[History] can help people, especially Native Americans, achieve something that had not quite been possible, namely they can tell their own story, but in telling their own story they also build their own strength as a people.

—Dave Warren, quoted in Roy T. Wortman,
"Dr. Dave Warren on Farming and Imparting American Indian History"

The Working Group on Indigenous Populations and the Declaration on the Rights of Indigenous Peoples now belong to history and to the personal story of all those who have contributed to the struggle for the recognition of Native rights. The Working Group on Indigenous Populations ceased its activities in 2006 and a new UN Permanent Forum on Indigenous Issues was set up in 2000 with a mandate to discuss Indigenous matters related to economic and social development, health, and human rights. Based in New York, the forum is made up of eight Indigenous individuals appointed by the president of the Economic and Social Council and eight members nominated by governments and elected by the Economic and Social Council.

Indigenous issues have been institutionalized and the geographical shift toward New York means that the pioneering period of Indigenous militancy in Geneva is over. Other UN agencies such as UNESCO, the ILO (International Labor Organization), the World Health Organization (WHO), and the World Intellectual Property Organization (WIPO), who have always covered Indigenous issues in their field of competence, have actively integrated Indigenous issues into their programs. They hold training programs for Indigenous students and organize panels on Indigenous issues. Many examples could be given of specific cases of sponsorship of Indigenous individuals and groups. UNESCO, as the United Nations Educational, Scientific and Cultural Organization, with a special expertise and commitment to cultural, religious, social, and educational rights, recognizes Indigenous cultures as part of the common heritage of humanity. Its Universal Declaration on Cultural Diversity, adopted unanimously by its member states in 2001, states that the protection and defense of this diversity is "an ethical imperative, inseparable from respect for human dignity" and implies "a commitment to human rights and fundamental freedoms . . . of Indigenous peoples" (Article 4).

During the first International Decade of the World's Indigenous Peoples (1995–2004) UNESCO designated a focal point and set up an intersectoral team to coordinate cooperation for the mainstreaming of Indigenous issues in its strategies and programs. In 2001 it organized a symposium titled Indigenous Identities: Oral, Written Expressions and New Technologies and a related book fair that brought together Native writers and publishers from all over the world. In 2004 N. Scott Momaday was named Artist for Peace at UNESCO, the only Indigenous representative, other than Rigoberta Menchú, to become an "ambassador" of Native rights.

Every year UNESCO participates in the Indigenous Fellowship Program, organized in concert with the Office of the United Nations High Commissioner for Human Rights and welcomes Native students for training programs. In 2008

it sponsored the Global Green Indigenous Festival organized in Santa Fe by the National Tribal Environment Council (NTEC). UNESCO also actively supports the protection of endangered languages and the mapping of Indigenous cultural resources carried out by the communities concerned.

Robert Tim Coulter's interview in chapter 14 offers us a balanced assessment of the importance of the work accomplished within the framework of the United Nations system. As director of a law firm with NGO credentials, he has over the years helped a number of newcomers. The Indian Law Resource Center was one of the first Native groups to achieve NGO status, with the Canadian Assembly of the First Nations and the International Indian Treaty Council. Coulter assesses the importance of the Declaration, and reminds us that it is the most comprehensive and significant of all instruments dealing with Indigenous peoples' rights. He has been one of the most fervent believers in the importance of the recognition of Indian rights on the international scene. For him the Declaration means a turning of the tide. Having followed all the steps that led to the final version of the text, Coulter remembers that the Working Group on Indigenous Populations achieved an extraordinary visibility in the UN system and "became the most active and heavily attended working group in UN history." He considers that, over the years, discussions and negotiations on legal grounds led, in many respects, to a better understanding between parties: "Naturally it was extremely difficult to persuade states that we deserved respect for our rights, but our steady presentation of evidence and sound argument . . . in time brought about astonishing changes in the behavior of states and wide agreement among states about most of the main principles of the draft declaration that was produced by the working group."

In 2004, the United Nations General Assembly proclaimed the Second International Decade of the World's Indigenous Peoples (2005–2014) to strengthen international cooperation for the solution of problems faced by Indigenous peoples in such areas as human rights, the environment, development, education, and health. It is currently estimated that Indigenous peoples represent some 350 million individuals or 5 percent of the world's population. Within this global context, considering the diversity of Indigenous cultures and histories and taking into account the ethical framework established within the United Nations system, international instruments can only provide general guidelines, while most of the practical work remains to be done at the regional and national level. But it was announced by the Permanent Forum on Indigenous issues, on December 22, 2010 that a UN World Conference on Indigenous Peoples would be held in 2014.

Coulter wants to see the promise of the Declaration become a reality and looks beyond its adoption by the United Nations: How do we make the Declaration work? What's the best way to continue to fight for laws, policies, and relationships taking into account the permanent presence of Indian Nations in the United States? He has been working on the adoption by the United States of a strong Declaration on the Rights of Indigenous Peoples in the Organization of American States.

The testimonies of those who have been part of this long diplomatic process provide a better understanding of the importance and limits of the declaration and of the significance of its implementation. According to Julian Burger, secretary of

the working group in Geneva, who has been committed to the defense of Indigenous rights throughout his career at the UN, what the Declaration offers is a framework for reconciliation and an agenda for policy discussion: "the UN system can play, as it often does, a valuable role as the catalyst for dialogue and understanding."[15]

Kenneth Deer's point of view, found in chapter 15, is also particularly interesting, because he was a journalist and an educator before becoming a talented Mohawk representative on the international scene. His quick understanding of UN rules and practices, his active participation in various panels and several UN bodies illustrate the extraordinary opportunities that have been offered to Native Americans on the international scene. Deer is not a lawyer, but he has had valuable experience in both activism and mediation. He acquired great visibility at the United Nations during the Oka Crisis (July 11–September 1990). As a former journalist he was chosen, inter alia, to become rapporteur of the UN workshop on Indigenous media in 2000. For him the negotiations in Geneva became an enriching experience, personally and professionally. Deer tells us that, when he arrived in 1986 in Geneva he had no experience of diplomacy and knew nobody on the international scene. But he quickly learned the ropes, was praised for his eloquence and his negotiating skills and soon had the opportunity to work in close cooperation with Erica Irene Daes, chairperson of the group. Deer and his wife Glenda became familiar figures at the United Nations, where they had the opportunity to fight for what they treasure most: the reappropriation of their culture, the defense of their language, and the transmission of their traditions. Deer also expresses a deep concern for the "survival" of his community. It seems to be the foundation of his personal commitments as he says, in concluding his interview: "it seems our destiny is to continue to struggle to survive. We must raise our children and our grandchildren to continue the struggle. If we ever stop struggling, then we will disappear."

CONCLUSION

> Half on the earth, half in the heart
> The remedies for all our pains
> Wait for the songs of healing
> —Joseph Bruchac, in Kenneth Lincoln, *Native American Renaissance*

Through the various testimonies brought together in this volume, and the personal stories that shed some singular light on major sociopolitical and cultural developments at the end of the twentieth century and the first decade of the twenty-first century, a polyphony of voices emerges, illustrating important aspects of the Native presence at the national and international level. As Vine Deloria Jr. announced in the 1980s an "articulate elite" has attempted to broker cultural changes.[16] In many ways, their creativity had led to new representations of Native Americans in mainstream society. All the contributors to this volume share with us, in the following pages, their multifaceted contribution to collective memory and to history.

Conversation with Gerald Vizenor,
series editor, poet, novelist, and art critic

Joëlle Rostkowski: You have made your reputation as one of the most prominent Native intellectuals of your generation, as a journalist, essayist, poet, novelist, and university professor. Having covered so much ground, and, as you have so much experience in Native communities, could you explain the accomplishments of your eclectic career?

Gerald Vizenor: Native American consciousness and the traces and stories of natural reason are mostly in the blood, innate, and sometimes visionary. Native descent can be a prominent source of confidence, along with cultural and family stories, and yet the politics of blood is never easy to unravel in Native associations. This bloody liquid arithmetic is not enviable or clearly acknowledged by anyone, and certainly not as a specialist on Native subjects.

Looking back to the major events that have marked my generation, clearly the most productive course was to be eclectic, to acquire a wide experience in various fields. I had no career plan, in other words. I was ambitious, driven by curiosity, and with a certain potential to establish myself as an author. I was ready to take on any duties and jobs connected with native issues and consciousness.

My accomplishments, and everything that happened to me in the first thirty years of my life, was by coincidence, clearly by chance associations, rather than through any deliberate preparation for a career. On the other hand, maybe it was inevitable that I became a journalist for the *Minneapolis Tribune* in the late 1960s. I had returned from military service in Japan, studied at New York University for one year, graduated from the University of Minnesota, and found myself at the center of radical movements. I organized a protest against the Bureau of Indian Affairs in Minneapolis, and that was the start of my active service in the native urban community.

Gerald Vizenor *(Photo by Laura Hall)*

I resisted the patrons of sympathy, those who found personal pleasure and authority in working with Natives as victims. I wanted to develop at the time some sense of survivance, and community structures that could help poor people in the area. Yes, my idea and philosophical sense of survivance was appreciated very early in my life and matured in the military and during my time as an advocate on the streets.

I wanted to create a place where Natives could count on an advocate to find medical care, jobs, and simply assistance in finding a place to stay for the night. Many Natives arrived in the city with ambition and ideals only to be discouraged by the customary social service agencies.

I volunteered as an advocate for several years in the Elliot Park community and on Franklin Avenue in Minneapolis. That area of the city had an estimated population of some five thousand Natives, and was referred to as the largest reservation in the state.

I raised money for a social service center, but did not accept any salary during my years as an advocate. My sense of duty as an advocate was an act of conscience, and was not a source of income or a career choice. Advocacy in a poor, broken, and desperate community should never be a source of income or pleasure. I was there because my father and grandmother had once lived in the area, and because my grandmother struggled to keep the family together and to overcome the extreme experiences of poverty and cultural disrespect.

Gerald Vizenor with the French painter Pierre Cayol *(Photo by Laura Hall)*

I was a child when my family, grandmother, aunts, and uncles left the reservation and moved to a dilapidated downtown apartment a few blocks from Elliot Park. My father worked as a house painter and was active in a union, at the time, and was probably murdered because of his political associations with a labor union, and for his participation in the truckers' strike in Minneapolis.

My service as an advocate was difficult, to say the least, but not without humor and irony. Natives can deliver a tricky, ironic, and memorable story in the very bowels of poverty. So, you see, my service was heavy, but every day the most desperate and tragic situations were transformed by marvelous native stories and irony. I learned about survivance as an advocate on the streets at this time.

There were no direct or immediate rewards for my advocacy, and it would have been improper if there were, because people in need should not be obligated to show appreciation for emergency medical care, or for assistance in finding an apartment or a job. I became a major advocate and player in the lives of hundreds of families and individuals, many natives who had just arrived in the city from reservations, and many others who were in desperate need of medical care and housing. And, providing any social services was very difficult because of the lack of support and funds from other agencies.

I was an advocate for several years and then returned to graduate school, continued to write haiku poetry, and published two books about the dream songs and stories of the Anishinaabeg. I also edited and published a collection of essays and historical articles as a commemoration of the White Earth Reservation, *Escorts to White Earth, 1868 to 1968: One Hundred Year Reservation*. I distributed without cost several hundred copies of the book more than forty years ago on the reservation. *Escorts to White Earth* is now a rare book and costs more than four hundred dollars.

JR: Was it at this time that you had the idea of becoming a writer?

GV: I was about twelve years old when I first considered the idea and fantasy of becoming a writer. Well, not actually a practicing writer, but the mere curiosity and untutored questions of becoming a writer.

I had read a pulp fiction adventure novel and thought about being a writer. I thought at the time that it might be easy to write a pulpy adventure story. I also thought about the business, only the business, of writing for newspapers at the time. I was hired, about a year later, at age thirteen, one of my first real jobs, to deliver the daily *Minneapolis Journal*. When that paper failed I was hired to deliver the prominent *Minneapolis Tribune*, a morning paper, and the *Minneapolis Star*, the evening paper. I also delivered the Sunday paper. I worked seven days a week in the early morning, and late in the afternoon, and on Sunday morning delivering papers to more than a hundred subscribers on my six-block route in north Minneapolis. I also made the rounds of my customers to collect money for the papers every two weeks. I could only have imagined at the time that less than twenty years later I would become a journalist, and then an editorial writer, for the *Minneapolis Tribune*. Nothing was ever really planned as a career.

My experiences and opportunities were realized only by coincidence, by the pleasure of chance. The *Minneapolis Journal* needed a delivery boy in my neighborhood. I was there on the street at the right moment, and ready to work. Then, a few months later, that newspaper was bought out. The *Minneapolis Star* and *Tribune* continued to employ the delivery boys who had worked for the *Journal*.

JR: So, as a boy on your first job you experienced the failure of a newspaper. Did you imagine that you would advance from a delivery boy to a journalist at the same newspaper?

GV: No, that was not even a fantasy. I watched journalists at events and accidents but had no conception of the actual writing process for a newspaper. I know—my experiences and careers are hard to believe as mere chance. I delivered newspapers for about two years and then less than twenty years later became a journalist for the same company. Even more remarkable is that my family published *The Progress*, the first newspaper published more than a century ago on the White Earth Reservation. Someone might wonder if there was more than chance in my experiences as a delivery boy and later as a journalist. Perhaps my connection with newspapers was inherited, a native destiny.

JR: When did you serve in the military?

GV: I actually served twice in the United States Army. I lied about my age and enlisted in the Minnesota National Guard. I was fifteen years old at the time, and had quit my newspaper route only a few months before my enlistment. Yes, I know, it is hard to believe that I was only fifteen years old, and that my decision to enlist was independent. Not one of my friends at the time would enlist with me. I was paid as a private and attended monthly training sessions at the Minneapolis Armory.

That summer, during the annual two weeks of intensive tactical training, the United States and United Nations entered the Korean War, on June 20, 1950. A few months later my National Guard unit was activated for service in Korea. The commanding officer, apparently aware of my age, made me an offer to either activate with the unit for combat duty in Korea or accept an honorable discharge. I was exceedingly proud, at the time, to have an honorable discharge at age sixteen, after about one year of service.

Two years later, on my eighteenth birthday, October 22, 1952, I quit high school and enlisted in the United States Army. My basic sixteen weeks of combat training were at Fort Knox, Kentucky. I completed training and was immediately assigned to combat duty in Korea. The troop ship arrived in Yokohama Bay, on the way to Incheon, Korea, in April 1953. Twice daily, from the top of the alphabet, soldiers were named and flown to the front lines in Korea.

Luckily, by the time the muster reached the twentieth letter of the alphabet, the Ts, the flights had ended. I was transferred with the bottom of the alphabet to serve in a tank battalion in the First Cavalry Division at Camp Chitose, Hokkaido, Japan. I met native Ainu on Hokkaido and was moved by their cultural association with bears. This reminded me of the obvious totemic connection of bears and the Anishinaabe. I was saved from combat duty by chance, only because my name was at the end of the alphabet.

The Korean armistice was signed on June 27, 1953. My service was entirely in Japan.

JR: You have written about Japanese haiku, art, and culture, and how imagistic poetry influenced your own work. What inspired you to pursue this form of poetry?

GV: The images of haiku are instant, an immediate poetic heartbeat, an image of a natural scene or ironic situation. I was impressed that ordinary people in Japan celebrated haiku poets, and quoted from their work. This ordinary experience of poetry was not strained by academic interpretations or pretensions, and there was heartfelt appreciation of many poets. Matsuo Basho, Issa, Buson, and many other haiku poets, for instance, were recognized and honored by ordinary people. So, my first experience was the immediate pleasure of imagistic poetry, and without any academic preparation. Poetry was a desperate subject in my public school experience, an imported literature that required a course of admission, and that course was a cultural division. I was on the outside of literature in public schools, and on the inside of imagistic poetry in Japan. I must be concerned here about oversimplification, that is, the romantic reduction of my experience and inspiration of haiku poetry.

So, this story may be a more reasonable description of how haiku poetry inspired me. My second duty post, after Hokkaido, was at Sendai, a few hours by train north of Tokyo. Matsushima Bay is nearby, a beautiful spectacle of many, many rocky pine islands in the bay.

I visited Matsushima several times, and on one occasion the full moon rose over the islands and the bay, the very same scene that Matsuo Basho observed three centuries earlier. He wrote about the moon and the beauty of the pine islands of Matsushima in "Narrow Road to the Deep North."

Basho in earlier poems created brief images that inspired an entire scene, a sentiment of natural reason, and, at times, a precise tease of traditions.

> ancient pond
> frog leaps
> sound of water

The conventions of a pensive culture and the serene practices of a reverent tradition are ruffled, or not, by a common frog that leaps into an ancient pond. The scene of ruffled water is a natural image of chance and impermanence. I understood these images, themes, sentiments, and the meditative philosophies of chance and impermanence, and without the burdens of academic performance. These experiences in Japan provided me with the confidence to seriously consider poetry and literature. The second significant influence of haiku was cultural and comparative, that is, the imagistic practices of haiku were similar to the native dream songs of the Anishinaabeg. I had heard the songs, and the stories of the songs, but had not made the critical imagistic connections with native dream song images until my experiences with haiku in Japan.

The imagistic associations of haiku and dreams songs are more synonymous than not, but there are obvious distinctions. Anishinaabe dream songs use first-person pronouns. The images of haiku, however, are seldom conveyed in a personal voice. Native and haiku images are natural reason and more about survivance than misery or victimry. One Anishinaabe dreamer, for instance, sang, "the sky loves to hear my voice." My favorite dream song image is ironic. A native woman who was not very attractive created this song, "I am as beautiful as the roses."

JR: When did you publish your first book of original haiku?

GV: I started to write haiku poems, and longer imagistic poems, in Japan. My first collection of haiku poems, *Raising the Moon Vines*, was published in 1964. I have published six books of original haiku poems, including *Matsushima: Pine Islands*, in the past thirty some years. Many of my longer poems, especially those recently published in *Almost Ashore*, are imagistic and concise, and reveal the influence and association of the haiku tradition.

JR: Did you return to Minnesota when you were discharged?

GV: Yes, but not for long. I was honorably discharged in August 1955 and returned to Minnesota long enough to visit with family and friends. I had been accepted to study at a radio and television engineering program in Washington, D.C. So, I bought a car and drove to the Capitol.

Meanwhile, I visited friends from the military in New York City. Mark Sullivan, a friend from the military, who had been discharged about the same time, invited me to study at New York University. I completed my first year there, dropped the idea of engineering and took up literature, and then returned with advanced academic standing to the University of Minnesota.

JR: Who were the authors that influenced you at the time?

GV: Thomas Wolfe, John Steinbeck, Jack London, and Nikos Kazantzakis, at first, and later on the translations of *The Stranger*, *The Fall*, and *The Plague* by Albert Camus. I was totally transformed by the novel *Look Homeward, Angel*, and by an anthology, *A Stone, a Leaf, a Door* by Wolfe. I was eighteen years old and truly, literally transformed, actually transported by the novels of Thomas Wolfe. I found a copy of *A Stone, a Leaf, a Door* on the shelf of a military library at Camp Sendai, Japan, and read the entire book leaning against the bookcase.

The Odyssey: A Modern Sequel by Nikos Kazantzakis has always inspired me, and the poem continues to stimulate me to this day. I am working on a long family poem in a similar style. These were some of my first memorable literary impressions and transformations.

Later, at the University of Minnesota, I was influenced by the philosophy of nihilism in *The Stranger* by Camus. Now, the problems of translation have become a significant part of my appreciation and critique of the novel, and, of course, nihilism must be compared to my fierce sentiments of native survivance, a sense of resistance and presence over absence, and the repudiation of victimry.

I was lucky once again, and by chance, to study with Eda Lou Walton, a marvelous poet and professor at New York University. She seemed to appreciate my innocence, actually my curiosity and awkwardness, as a writer. She asked me about the writers who had influenced me. I mentioned Thomas Wolfe, of course, but she did not seem to share my enthusiasm for his figurative stretch of diction and description. She never questioned, however, my personal choice of authors. Rather, she supported and stimulated my impressions of literature.

Thomas Wolfe and Eda Lou Walton, some thirty years later, had occupied the same academic office when they taught at New York University. Walton was supportive and sharply critical at the same time, but she encouraged me to pursuing creative writing. The unions of chance continued when she told me to study at the University of New Mexico. She had taught literature at New Mexico, associated with many women writers in the state, and published a book of native poetry. She advised me as a native to live and write in New Mexico. I was named a Distinguished Professor of American Studies at the University of New Mexico almost fifty years later.

I learned later that Eda Lou Walton had also taught at the University of California, Berkeley. So, the memories of my very best writing teacher are associated with three places and institutions, New York, Berkeley, and Albuquerque. Walton is my sense of presence in many places. I retired as Emeritus Professor in American Studies from Berkeley.

JR: You started teaching at the University of California, Berkeley, in 1976, and at about the same time your first novel, Bearheart, was published and rapidly became a success.

GV: Yes, *Bearheart* and Berkeley were heady experiences at the time, the challenge of teaching at a great university, and critical attention for a very controversial novel. *Bearheart*, the story of natives, reservation pilgrims, on the road of horror and travail after the end of gasoline, scared some readers and enchanted others. The late seventies was a time of strained humor, political comedy, and unintended irony. San Francisco became a new congress of sexual independence. Gurus arrived from the ancient world with arcane chants, diets, venture strategies, and manicured hands and perfectly formed feet. Cults emerged and flower children were triumphant. Some cults, however, turned fascist and exploited the spirit.

I wrote *Bearheart* in two years during a serious petroleum shortage in the country, and the novel was published in a time of social and cultural dissociations. I provided no apologies to anyone for the extreme scenes in the novel, scenes of gruesome violence over the possession of a few gallons of gasoline. Newspapers reported similar situations, but not with the detailed description of cruelty and violence. Cars were abandoned in the novel, interstate highways were deserted, and wanderers were captures by fascists at rest stops.

So, Berkeley was an ironic academic paradise of acacia and magnolia in bloom, and, at the same time, *Bearheart* was published, an ominous novel about the extreme social disintegration of the country in search for gasoline. I could not easily overcome the contradictions of these experiences by the customary poses of native students and identity politics.

I had never been anywhere warm in the winter, so the flower of acacia and magnolia was a pleasurable distraction that winter of my chance connections and appointment to teach in native American studies at Berkeley.

JR: Over the last few years you have been very active in the literary field, both as a novelist, *Hiroshima Bugi: Atomu 57* (2003), *Chancers* (2007), *Father Meme* (2008), and *Shrouds of White Earth* (2010), and also as an editor and essayist, *Survivance: Narratives of Native Presence* (2008), *Native Storiers* and *Native Liberty: Natural Reason and Cultural Survivance* (2009). You have published more than thirty books, but recently you seem to be very focused, creative, and productive.

GV: Yes, the last few years have been very productive, fiction and critical essays. The concentration of two novels, however, extends over many more years of research and reading.

Father Meme, for instance, was a very complicated and heartfelt narrative, as you know, the narrative of three altar boys sexually abused by a Catholic priest on a reservation in Minnesota. I read widely, researched the subject for more than two years, and considered the recent court decision against individual priests and bishops at Catholic Diocese in the United States. The court documents and other investigative information were about priests who were moved from one parish to another to avoid notice and prosecution, and hardly any reports were about the thousands of Natives who had been abused by priests on reservations. The Catholic Church more often than not avoided the responsibilities of priestly abuse and transferred these sexual predators to other communities, and to Indian reservations around the country. The Church and bishops conspired to conceal a crime, and the crime of conspiracy was not within the statute of limitations. The crimes of sexual abuse had a statute of limitations, and many priests escaped prosecution in this way. Finally, newspapers reported on the lawsuits and the decisions of the courts, but not about the abuse of natives on reservations.

JR: And was that the reason you wrote *Father Meme*?

GV: Yes, but my dedication to the subject and literary practices considered more than the absence of investigative reports about the abuse of Natives. I was determined in my novel to present native altar boys, abused by a priest, in the sentiments of survivance, not victimry. I created a narrative about how the native altar boys tried to outwit and outmaneuver the priest, rather than the familiar narratives of native victimry. The altar boys in my novel were nurtured by relatives and encouraged to practice native trickery to distract the abusive priest, and to drive him away from the reservation. The imaginative and traditional practices of the altar boys, however, did not scare the priest to leave. Instead, the priest seemed to become even more abusive and evil. So, the altar boys performed a ritual sacrifice of the priest, including the Fourteen Torments based on the Stations of the Cross. The native community was convinced that the priest was so wicked that no one would ever notice or worry that he was missing, not even the Catholic Church. Indeed, in the narrative, no one missed the abusive priest, and no crime was ever reported on the reservation.

JR: I understand that you struggled for more than a year with the point of view and literary style of the novel.

GV: The point of view of the novel became a very serious problem for me. I could not bring myself to write as an omniscient narrator, because no author could know that much about the abuses of priests on reservations, and omniscience was not an acceptable narrative for my novel. I first tried to write in the first person, but that point of view was both deceptive and disingenuous at the same time. I could not in good conscience create a narrative of sexual abuse in the first-person point of view.

Limited omniscience was never a narrative possibility, because, in my view, it was insincere. The sentiments of omniscience are monotheistic and suggest victimry. The narrator would demonstrate only limited knowledge, but to hold back on some experience and information was doubly insincere, and false. I wrote many experimental pages, but the first- and third-person narratives were not acceptable. I was prepared to actually abandon the entire project.

Some months later, the second-person point of view came to mind in an unrelated project. I was considering *The Plague* and *The Stranger* by Albert Camus for an essay, and remembered reading, as a college sophomore, *The Fall* by Camus, a short novel in the second-person point of view. I reread *The Fall* in translation and found my point of view for *Father Meme*. The narrator, a retired native journalist, similar to my own experience, returns to the reservation and tells his story to a visiting French historian and constitutional scholar. She is studying the constitutions of native reservations. The narrator tells the scholar about his experience as an altar boy, the abuse of the priest, and the gruesome sacrifice of the priest in an ice fishing house on Wiindigoo Lake.

The narrator reveals certain responses of the scholar by way of the second-person point of view. Once I found my style, the second person, after so many experiments, the narrative almost wrote itself over a concentrated period of about six months.

JR: Were you writing *Father Meme*, essays for you new collection, *Native Liberty*, editing essays for *Survivance*, and teaching all at the same time?

GV: Yes, teaching is almost always stimulating, but not in this instance. The subject of the novel was not something that I could present or reasonably discuss in lectures or seminars, except, of course, in a much larger context of the subject, the court proceedings and documents of priestly abuse. The critical subject of an essay, on the other hand, is much easier to consider in a seminar. I often try to develop and tease my theoretical ideas in graduate seminars, and sometimes in undergraduate lecture courses.

JR: *Survivance* was published in the same year as *Father Meme*. How were you able to separate these two literary activities?

GV: I had already written about the concept and general theory of survivance, that is a sentiment and philosophy that would celebrate presence over historical absence. Survivance is the political and ecstatic courage of resistance over the mundane themes of victimry. I was determined to write a definitive essay on survivance, and then to invite scholars to use my ideas and theoretical considerations of survivance in an original essay about native literature or history. I was very pleased by the positive responses of so many distinguished scholars, and impressed by the actual essays they wrote for the publication of *Survivance* by the University of Nebraska Press. Contributors include the late Karl Kroeber, Helmbrecht Breinig, Deborah Madsen, A. Robert Lee, Arnold Krupat, Susan Bernardin, Alan Velie, Diane Glancy, James Mackay, Takayuki Tatsumi, Jace Weaver, and many other literary scholars. My introductory essay concentrated on the aesthetics of survivance, the literary theory, philosophy, and practice.

JR: Could you briefly describe more specifically what you mean by survivance?

GV: Yes, and my description here, in response to your question, has been derived mostly from the first paragraph of my introductory essay on the subject. The theories of survivance are elusive, as you know, obscure, and imprecise by definition and translation in comparative literature and history. The idea and sentiment of survivance, however, is invariably true and just in native literary practices. The nature, or natural reason, of survivance is unmistakable in native stories, remembrance, traditions, and clearly observable in narrative resistance. The character of survivance creates a sense of native presence, a critical, active presence and resistance, over absence, historical and cultural absence, nihility, and victimry.

Yes, native survivance is an active sense of presence over absence, and survivance is the continuance of stories, not a mere reaction, however pertinent reactions might be in cultural studies. Survivance is much greater than the right of a survivable name.

Survivance stories, and this is my primary practice in literature, are renunciations of dominance, detractions, the unbearable sentiments of tragedy, and the legacy of victimry. Survivance, as you know, is the heritable right of succession or reversion of an estate, and, in the course of international declarations of human rights, a narrative estate of native survivance.

JR: Recently you turned to writing critical and interpretative essays about Native artists. Is this a shift in your focus and work?

GV: Yes, a recent concentration, you might say, but not my first consideration of native artistic production. I have taught about native art, and have been critical of the cultural representations of native art imposed by social scientists. The *soi-disant ledger* artists, for instance, those native artists who were prisoners at Fort Marion, Florida, were observed as the untutored creators of cultural scenes and representations. The blue, green, and red horses in flight, and other images created by these artists, are visionary not naturalistic, primitive, or representational. Many European artists were inspired by these visionary native paintings, those that were presented in early museums. European artists were reviewed as innovative, cubist, modernist, but the scenes created by native artists were set by definitions of primitivism.

The irony is that native artists anticipated cubism and modernism.

I have written interpretive essays about two Anishinaabe artists, George Morrison and David Bradley. The acknowledged irony of native art in the nineteenth century was reversed, a double irony, in the recognition of the brilliant abstract expressionist art by George Morrison. The cultural simulations of native art that were established by curators, and the paintings by those native artists who departed from the simulations, were excluded from museum exhibitions. Oscar Howe, George Morrison, and other native artists were excluded from exhibitions because their art was abstract and expressionistic, not native in the view of certain curators.

George Morrison earned international recognition for his abstract expressionist paintings. His work has been exhibited with other distinguished abstract painters in New York, and in museums around the country, but his artistic expressions were not accepted as native art until the late 1960s. That slight of curatorial dominance was fully overcome by the presentation and celebration of huge abstract expressionist paintings by George Morrison at the Inaugural Exhibition of the Smithsonian National Museum of American Indian in Washington, D.C., in 2004.

I wrote the essay on Morrison for the inaugural exhibition catalogue, "George Morrison: Anishinaabe Expressionism at Red Rock," in *Native Modernism: The Art of George Morrison and Allan Houser.* I wrote, "George Morrison teased the elusive hues and mighty blaze of colors, the rise and weave of wood, and the ancient creases of stone. He envisioned an eternal horizon in his memorable creations, an aesthetic meditation on the tones of nature and natural liberty."

George Morrison died at age eighty on April 17, 2000, in Grand Marais, Minnesota. Mary Abbe reported in the *Minneapolis Star Tribune* that Morrison was "one of Minnesota's most distinguished and beloved artists." She observed and compared the paintings of Morrison with those of Claude Monet, the "famous impressionist paintings of the Seine River," and the abstract expressionist scenes of Lake Superior by George Morrison. The horizon lines shimmered over the lake in his paintings, the trace and magic of nature, not the impressions of a river in Paris.

David Bradley creates bright, brilliant, meticulous, and ironic native narratives of familiar scenes in Minnesota and New Mexico. My essay "Bradlarian Baroque: The Narrative Art of David Bradley" was published in the retrospective exhibition *David Bradley: Restless Native, The Journey* at the Nicolaysen Art Museum in Casper, Wyoming, 2009. Bradley's baroque, ironic, and detailed narrative style, and his use of bold, bright colors, has been resisted by certain curators. Native painters must be aware of the intense politics of curators to survive as artists. Bradley was aware, of course, but he actually provoked the politics by creating ironic narratives and images of some of those very curators and fanciers who perpetuated the nasty politics of native art.

Bradley is an ironic native storier with paint. I wrote in the exhibition catalogue that Bradley creates figures that are slightly contorted, whimsical, wittingly eccentric, and freaky at times, and with a sense of ironic motion in the bright colors, composition, and painterly features.

Santa Fe Indian Market, for instance, shows a gathering of zany characters: a native clown on a skateboard with a watermelon, dogs, birds, a buffalo head, a ghostly arm reaching out of a manhole for money, decorative cowboy boots under a table, an ersatz Sikh, and four people queued with fists of money to buy native pottery, and other simulated, ironic characters gathering on one afternoon at the Plaza in Santa Fe, New Mexico.

Bradley never hesitates to declare that art is liberty. He is a painter of continental liberty, and his narrative scenes liberate and heal by images, stories, and irony.

JR: UNESCO invited you, in June 2009, to attend an international seminar on art, "What Can Art Still Do?" This seminar was in preparation of the second World Conference on Arts Education to be held in Seoul, Korean, in 2010. Could you comment on the content of your presentation at the international seminar?

GV: My presentation integrated critical ideas about native art practices and literary art. I pointed out how native art has been simulated and classified as cultural representations rather than discussed as artistic creation. The *ledger* art painters, and hide painters, for instance, were visionary artists. Most of these native artists created scenes from memory, and the images of memory are not realistic portrayals.

Native abstract art surely preceded cubism, modernism, and other artistic movements in the world. Clearly the expectations of traditional native themes, such as realism, naturalism, and cultural representations were initiated by the pedagogy of Dorothy Dunn. She founded the Studio School as part of the Santa Fe Indian

School, in New Mexico, in 1932. Dunn advanced the notion that natives were innate artists.

Dunn proposed that native artists should not be distracted by the ideas and practice of landscape perspective, or by the abstract expressionism of modern art. So, she encouraged students to create outlines and flat colors to represent cultural traditions, not knowing at the time that many of those cultural traditions, sacred dances and ceremonies, were protected and representations were forbidden.

People around the world were encouraged to believe that native art was an insight into traditions, a marvellous expression of primitivism and cultural reality. Fritz Scholder, a native artist, broke away from the representational style of native art and practiced abstract figuration and expressionism. He rejected the simulated images and painted abstract portrayals of Natives.

Scholder sold his huge abstract paintings in New York City. That changed forever the way most people reviewed and understood the artistic production of native artists.

Native abstract expressionist paintings presented at the time in exhibitions and museums seemed to be immediately understood by most curators and art historians. Slowly, the manifest cultural and representational images were retired, except, of course, the treasures of certain nostalgic museum curators. This breakthrough, from innate traditional art to expressionism, however, has not been similarly appreciated in native literary art. I mean, the innovative novels and short stories by native writers are not appreciated in the same was as native expressionistic paintings.

French innovative literary artists of the nouveau roman have inspired and influenced authors around the world, including many native novelists. Yet, many publishers seem to be adverse to innovative nouveau roman native authors, except, of course, certain university publishers. Most international publishers consider for translation the more commercial native novels that simulate tragic victimry over survivance, and romantic notions about warrior cultures. These commercial novels are not reliable representations of native traditions. Rather, the commercial narratives are simulations of culture, and the tragic and romantic themes of victimry.

Some contemporary native writers might look back to the great authors of innovative literature, the nouveau roman, and publishers might do the same, consider in translation the innovative narratives of native authors.

Native literature, for the first time in literary history, can be clearly discussed and compared in two categories: native literary art and native commercial fiction.

These two styles of literature require the same critical scrutiny as any other literature. The categories are not essential or absolute, of course, and are used only for purposes of comparative discussions. Native commercial fiction finds a much wider audience because the themes and style of the narratives focus more on tragic victimry, that is, the popular notions of terminal traditions and cultures. Native literary art, the innovative novelist and storiers of the native "nouveau roman," more often create scenes of survivance, that is, the metaphors and tropisms of chance and irony. Native cultures and traditional practices are not easily understood by outsiders, and the mysteries of any culture cannot be delivered by commercial representations. Native literary artists create narrative scenes that are innovative and ironic.

CONTRIBUTION TO THE
WHITE EARTH RESERVATION CONSTITUTION

JR: Recently you were a delegate to the White Earth Reservation Constitutional Convention, and you wrote the new Constitution of the White Earth Nation. Did your extensive experience as a creative writer and essayist make it easier to write a constitution?

GV: Yes, my experience as a writer was useful, but more important was the concentration of native ideas in my essays. Narrative style was not that critical, at first, but the diverse native subjects of my essays became a significant source of information in writing the new constitution. This experience, to actually write a constitution, was an extraordinary responsibility. How many people are asked to create a narrative constitution? Not many, and it was my absolute duty to prepare a document that would provide and protect the ideals, rights, and sovereignty of Natives, and, at the same time, to declare a sense of Native continental survivance and liberty.

I was one of forty Natives nominated as delegates to convene and discuss the content of a proposed constitution. There were four Constitutional Conventions held for two days each at the Shooting Star Casino on the White Earth Reservation. The sworn delegates duly ratified the Constitution of the White Earth Nation on April 2, 2009, at the last Constitutional Convention. The ratification was by secret ballots of twenty-four delegates present. Sixteen delegates voted for ratification, and eight delegates voted against the ratification. The ratification was passed by a simple majority of delegates present.

One of the most contentious issues discussed by the delegates during the four Constitutional Conventions was the consideration and continuation of the notion of arithmetic blood quantum to determine native membership of the White Earth Reservation. The federal government foisted the dubious system of blood quantum on the tribal government half a century ago. Jill Doerfler, who studied the early tribal documents for her doctoral dissertation, pointed out that tribal leaders had resisted the imposition of the bloody racial arithmetic to decide membership of the reservation, and capitulated only when the federal government threatened the termination of the reservation. The majority of delegates voted to determine citizenship by direct family descent based on the first families of the White Earth Reservation. These were the native families that were enumerated at the time the reservation was established by the Treaty of March 19, 1867.

The contention between delegates over the issue of family descent and blood quantum to determine citizenship in the White Earth Nation could not be equitably resolved at the Constitutional Conventions. So, the resolution to the diverse positions that would determine citizenship was left to me as the writer.

I presented two paragraphs, or two separate articles that represented the specific interests of the delegates, those who promoted a new constitution based on family descent, and those delegates who were concerned about services based on blood quantum and would not abandon the federal system as a measure of citizenship.

CITIZENS OF THE WHITE EARTH NATION
(CHAPTER 2)

Article 1

Citizens of the White Earth Nation shall be descendants of Anishinaabeg families and related by linear descent to enrolled members of the White Earth Reservation and Nation, according to genealogical documents, treaties and other agreements with the government of the United States.

Article 2

Services and entitlements provided by government agencies to citizens, otherwise designated members of the White Earth Nation, shall be defined according to treaties, trusts, and diplomatic agreements, state and federal laws, rules and regulations, and in policies and procedures established by the government of the White Earth Nation.

PREAMBLE TO THE CONSTITUTION
OF THE WHITE EARTH NATION

The Anishinaabeg of the White Earth Nation are the successors of a great tradition of continental liberty, a native constitution of families, totemic associations. The Anishinaabeg create stories of natural reason, of courage, loyalty, humor, spiritual inspiration, survivance, reciprocal altruism, and native cultural sovereignty.

We the Anishinaabeg of the White Earth Nation in order to secure an inherent and essential sovereignty, to promote traditions of liberty, justice, and peace, and reserve common resources, and to ensure the inalienable rights of native governance for our posterity, do constitute, ordain and establish this Constitution of the White Earth Nation.

I was nominated three months later to prepare the Bylaws of Governance for the White Earth Nation, that is, the actual procedures by which the elected government and judiciary shall carry out the provisions of the Constitution of the White Earth Nation. The Bylaws were adopted on July 25, 2009.

The Preamble to the Constitution of the White Earth Nation recounts and conveys native values and sentiments of governance and sovereignty. The first paragraph of the Preamble proclaims the traditional principles and ethics of native families, totemic associations, survivance, and cultural sovereignty. The second paragraph of the Preamble proclaims the protection of native rights, justice, and peace.

CHAPTER ONE

N. Scott Momaday, poet, novelist, painter, and UNESCO Artist for Peace

N. Scott Momaday (Kiowa/Cherokee) likes to describe himself as a storyteller. As Charles L. Woodard has noted in *Ancestral Voice*, N. Scott Momaday's voice is "naturally, conversationally, the voice of his writings."[1] Conversations with him have a "literate resonance." Over the years our conversations have occurred in various places: Jemez, the family house, where his mother Natachee spent the last years of her life and where he felt in tune with the most minute nuances of the environment, but also Santa Fe, sometimes with his wife Barbara, and often in Paris, at UNESCO or in the Latin Quarter.

This interview is based upon many precious moments shared with him and his family. Over the years N. Scott Momaday has become, for many of his readers, collectors, and publishers, more than a famous writer. A "wordwalker," as he likes to say, a "word sender" as Black Elk called John Neihardt. But also a patriarch, a fatherly figure, an emissary of Native wisdom.[2]

> **In the spirit of hope**
> . . . We are present in our words
> We are alive in our words
> We are immortal in our words
> —Oklahoma City National Memorial, April 19, 2005

Joëlle Rostkowski: You have expressed your creativity in many different fields, mostly literary but also artistic and diplomatic. You have received the Pulitzer Prize for your novel *House Made of Dawn*, at a very early stage in your career, attracting attention to the literary creativity of Native Americans, paving the way for several generations of Native American novelists and poets. For many years you have been

N. Scott Momaday in Paris *(Photo by Nicolas Rostkowski)*

a professor of English and American Literature. Simultaneously you have become a painter whose work has been exhibited both in the United States and abroad (recently in Paris). In 2004 you were named Artist for Peace by UNESCO. Looking back at all those distinctions, how do you define yourself?

N. Scott Momaday: First and foremost, as a writer. And as an American Indian. My Indian background has been influential in all my endeavors. My identity—for me being Indian has been good—has been the foundation of my work. Already at a very early age I enjoyed playing with words, with the oral and the written language. My identity as a painter came later. My father was an artist and art was present in my life throughout my childhood. But I was already forty years old—I was then visiting the Soviet Union—when, suddenly, everything my father had taught me came to the surface.

I always enjoyed teaching. Teaching and writing strengthen each other. Exchanges with the students have kept my mind alive, and I always found dialogue with them very rewarding. I am associated with a number of educational organizations and I am still an active member on several educational boards, in particular the board of the School of Advanced Research. I am also delighted to have been appointed Artist for Peace by UNESCO. I have worked with Indigenous peoples in Siberia, Alaska, as well as in my own Kiowa community. I worked with my wife Barbara, a lawyer, who was very

N. Scott Momaday in Paris (UNESCO). Nomination ceremony as Artist for Peace (May 2004) with Koïchiro Matsuura (Director General) and Louise V. Oliver, US Representative to UNESCO. *(Courtesy of UNESCO/Michel Ravassard)*

supportive of my activities on the international scene, on a UNESCO project dealing with the transmission of knowledge at Rainy Mountain, the recording of oral tradition for the young generation. Being involved with activities concerning Indigenous peoples over the world has allowed me to share my knowledge and to broaden my perspective.

JR: Looking back at what you have achieved, do you feel that you have gone beyond your childhood dreams?

NSM: I feel I have exceeded my dreams. I wanted—first and foremost—to be a writer. It's a great satisfaction to have done it and to have achieved some recognition. I was the only child of educator parents. Looking back at my family, I remember my mother writing and my father painting. During my childhood I didn't keep my dreams secret. I shared them with my mother, who was very close to me and encouraged me. Actually both my parents trusted me and gave me great confidence. This is why nobody could ever make me feel inferior.

Beyond family influence, some teachers have been influential in my life, but not until I was in college and probably more in graduate school. I remember Yvor Winters, poet, critic, and professor of English literature at Stanford University, where I was a graduate student. He was a man of letters, and a bright star of his time (he died in 1968). He held a famous and influential position at the university and became a teacher to many poets of several generations. I used to show him my poems and we talked about them. He gave me some good advice and, thanks to him, I learned a lot about traditional forms in English and about American literary history.

JR: Do you remember when and how you decided to write your first novel?

NSM: It was a happy and creative period in my life. I remember clearly that I wrote the first part of *House Made of Dawn* in Jemez, in our family home. I wrote it rather confidently, with serenity, although I knew I would conjure up rather dramatic events in that story. At that time I had been sharing my time between teaching at Stanford and writing poetry.

I felt the need to expand myself, to extend the scope of my literary work. I think that, as a teenager, I was very deeply moved by the destiny of some of the veterans I came across at Jemez Pueblo. I somehow felt bound to write about them. *House Made of Dawn* was based upon painful memories of the people I encountered, desperate young men who slowly destroyed themselves through violence or alcohol or simply committed suicide.

I think that *House Made of Dawn* can be considered as the portrait of a lost generation. It is centered upon Pueblo culture but deals with historical events that have affected various tribes. Abel, my hero, is a broken man when he returns from the war. He has lost his sense of tribal identity and has experienced violence, discrimination, and spiritual emptiness in mainstream society. The novel's title comes from an old Navajo healing song: "House made of dawn, house made of evening light, house made of dark cloud." The story is also about healing. It's based upon the healing power of the environment and upon recollections of the beautiful, striking, and occasionally violent rituals that impressed me so deeply as a young man because I felt the power in them. Ceremonies reiterate personal and collective history, allowing participants to circle back to their origins and to restore themselves.

JR: In *The Way to Rainy Mountain*, a pilgrimage that takes you on the footsteps of your Kiowa ancestors, you explore Native history and embark on a spiritual journey. In *The Names* you conjure up the story of your family, Cherokee on your mother's side, Kiowa on your father's side. You evoke your happy childhood, deeply rooted in family traditions, but mostly spent on reservations away from Indians of your own tribes. You seem to have kept a delicate balance between remaining faithful to your tribal roots (you are still an active member of a Kiowa warrior society) and extending your concerns and your experience beyond the limits of a specific community and a specific country. You also seem to have mastered many different forms of written literature (fiction, poetry, theater), often referring to the power of words explicitly acknowledged in the oral tradition.

NSM: I believe in the power of words. For me words are intrinsically powerful. One should use words carefully. Traditional rituals remind us that words can be sent as visionary spirits, as medicine. Traditional storytellers and singers know that words can rid the body of sickness, capture the heart of a lover, subdue an enemy. And I consider myself a storyteller as well as a novelist or a poet because I know that when you tell a story, it comes alive. There are many ways to communicate with the audience: voice, rhythm, and silences in which words are anticipated or held on to.

As far as roots are concerned I always felt that I could remain faithful to my family history and the memory of older generations while broadening my knowledge and my experience through traveling, exploring new grounds. I am also an explorer. I have traveled extensively to Russia, Central Asia, onto the foothills of the Himalayas. I always enjoyed discovering other worlds, other ways, and different qualities of light, new angles of vision.

JR: Where there some important factors, unexpected key elements that you still remember as having had a strong influence in your life?

NSM: The time I spent in Russia was very important. I remember that I found a lot of energy for writing and drawing while I was there. Generally speaking the time that I spent abroad—whether it be Spain, Italy, France, to mention only some of my favorite European countries—has been deeply memorable. As for Central Asia, it has been the most exotic place I have visited and images of that part of the world remain as something strong, unforgettable.

JR: How do you view your literary career and the development of Native American literature during the last decades?

NSM: We have come a long way. At the heart of the American Indian oral tradition is a deep belief in the efficacy of language. Now that we communicate through the written word and mostly in English, this belief remains as strong as ever. Language is sacred. The writer recreates the world in words. And now that we see an increasing number of Native writers achieving recognition, through prose or poetry, they express their identity and share their memory with non-Indian readers.

I strongly believe that one of the most important developments in contemporary American literary history has been the emergence of the Native voice. The Native American literary scene is burgeoning. In 1969 I was lucky enough to achieve success with *House Made of Dawn*, and it brought me—and other young writers who followed in my footsteps—a lot of encouragement. For me, at that time, the knowledge that I could be published was the key factor. The Pulitzer Prize came as an unexpected reward. From then on a growing body of work developed, prose and poetry being natural forms of expression complementing each other.

I was pleased to see other very good writers asserting themselves: James Welch's first novel, *Winter in the Blood*, has become a classic story of reservation life. He has written a couple of other novels that are notable. Leslie Silko's *Ceremony* is a very skillful treatment of the contemporary Pueblo world. Gerald Vizenor is a brilliant trickster figure, who, since the publication of *Darkness in Saint Louis: Bearheart*, his first novel, has been very prolific and appears as the supreme ironist among American Indian writers of the twentieth century. Louise Erdrich has written successful novels, which evoke life in the Northern Plains. I also admire the work of the poet Simon Ortiz, of Linda Hogan. I like the poetry of Luci Tapahonso and enjoy the provocative narratives of Sherman Alexie. Over the last twenty or thirty years, Native writers have broken down barriers, they have made their "entrée" into the larger world.

Young people have more opportunities to go to college and to graduate from good universities. The language barrier has been an obstacle for many years. Thirty years ago students spoke broken English and now they can master communication, both in the literary field and on the political scene. Simultaneously there has been a movement toward safeguarding Native languages. Significant measures have been taken to teach languages still alive within the communities. Unfortunately some languages are lost beyond recovery but many are being revived. The Kiowa language, for example, is being taught at the University of Oklahoma.

JR: You seem to be quite optimistic about the future. Still you are very concerned with the new generation of Native Americans dropouts, estranged from their roots, cut off from the memory of older generations, too influenced by TV programs and dissatisfied with the materialism of mainstream America.

NSM: I am concerned about the transmission of knowledge. Very often, as I am aware through the observation of my own Kiowa community, there is poor communication between parents and children, because the parents are busy and tired, and also because television, in many homes, has replaced family communication. This is why I have created the Buffalo Trust, whose objective is to revive traditional culture, to reinforce the dialogue between generations; I want to foster the development of local archives where oral tradition could be preserved, native stories videotaped, and where young people could have access to computers, where they could listen to old tales told by elders and, in a very casual way, rediscover their roots.

American Indians are at a crossroads and I often feel discouraged when I see that we are still collectively and statistically well below standard in terms of health, income, and education. Alcohol and drugs destroy a lot of youngsters. The efforts to reinforce tribal values are varied and remarkable but they are inevitably diluted because of intermarriage. Even when two persons of different tribal backgrounds get married and have a family, it's difficult to transmit two traditions and to practice two Native languages while learning English at the same time.

Still the example of the Pequot Indians who managed successfully to restore their tribe, to reconstruct their genealogy and their history, is encouraging. They are prosperous because of the casino, but they have been able to build an interesting museum and they have established a system of scholarships for the young generation. Many people have been worrying about the casinos on Indian land. But it is also notable that in New Mexico, many pueblo tribes make use of them to organize art shows and support local artists.

JR: Your determination to reach out to the younger generation and to look beyond individual literary success seems to apply to your own family. You have four daughters, several grandchildren, and you are very close to them. Has your experience as a father been important for you?

NSM: I strongly believe it has been my greatest accomplishment. I have four beautiful and talented daughters and eight grandchildren. The relationship we have established over the years is very strong, although two of my daughters do not live in New Mexico. Family relationships are of utmost importance in my life. I consider them as my greatest success.

WORLD POETRY DAY

March 21st 2010
Theme:
"The Words of Nature, the Nature of Words"
Message sent by Scott Momaday, read at UNESCO (Paris) and at the
United Nations (New York)

As a UNESCO Artist for Peace, I am honored and delighted to participate in the celebration of World Poetry Day. I regard poetry as the highest expression of literature, and I am greatly pleased to know that it is so regarded around the world. Not only is a poem a statement concerning the human condition composed in verse, but at its best it is a profound statement, one that enables us to know who, and where, and what we are in relation to the storm of distraction that surrounds us. Poetry is ancient, perhaps as old as language itself, and it stands among the greatest achievements of the human mind and heart. It is our best legacy. It is our immortality.

I would like to share with you one of my recent poems:

THE SNOW MARE

> In my dream, a blue mare loping,
>
> Pewter on a porcelain field, away.
>
> There are bursts of soft commotion
>
> Where her hooves drive in the drifts,
>
> And as dusk ebbs on the plane of night,
>
> She shears the web of winter,
>
> And on the far, blind side
>
> She is no more. I behold nothing,
>
> Wherein the mare dissolves in memory,
>
> Beyond the burden of being.

—N. Scott Momaday

CHAPTER TWO

Suzan Harjo, policy advocate, journalist, essayist, and poet

Suzan Harjo (Muscogee/Cheyenne) is an extraordinary woman. Beautiful, strong. She is a warrior who has won many battles and is still leading many fights for religious freedom, peace, and sacred natural places. She is a poet, writer, curator, lecturer, and policy advocate, who has helped Native nations recover more than one million acres of land. Suzan has developed key federal Indian laws since the late 1960s, and has been instrumental in national policy advances concerning the protection of Native American cultures. She is president and executive director of the Morning Star Institute, a national Indian rights organization founded in 1984. An award-winning columnist, she writes for leading American Indian publications. Her articles have been widely published in anthologies, and her essay entitled *Redskins, Savages, and Other Indian Enemies: A Historical Overview of American Indian Media Coverage of Native Peoples*, is fiery, precise, and striking, just like her.[1]

Joëlle Rostkowski: How would you like to define yourself? You have been active in so many different fields, what is the definition that would correspond to what you do now and what you have accomplished in the past?

Suzan Harjo: I am a writer. I like to write in different ways—poetry, journalism, federal Indian law, history, speeches, arts, and social criticism. It's much like gardening—you work with the soil, plant, leave it alone to grow, then return to trim and admire.

A lot of things write themselves; others are written for the cause and are not meant to carry your name. Most people don't know what I've written or what I've made happen. The movements of the peoples are more important than credit. Some call me a radical, but my radical ideas and writings have been signed into law by every American president since Nixon. That kind of writing is for history and for the good.

Suzan Harjo *(Photo by Nicolas Rostkowski)*

JR: During your childhood did you ever dream of doing what you do now?

SH: I always knew I was a writer. Everybody told me that. During my childhood, I also knew I was a hunter, a swimmer, a dancer, a singer. My big, extended family and other teachers taught me to develop those talents and to be brave. It never occurred to me there were things I couldn't do. They also told me that white people would try to break my spirit, just as they had twisted history. My family understood the role of oral history, of writing things right through the memory of the people concerned.

I was always prepared for outsiders to try to make me and our Native peoples into lesser beings, and to resist them and to prevail. Our great prophet, Sweet Medicine, who reordered Cheyenne society, foretold the coming of white people. He said they'd make train tracks, roads, and other lines across Mother Earth that would look like a massive web of a spider, a *veho*. He said to our people: "Don't let the *veho* mark you, enmesh you, or crawl near you."

My parents and grandparents gave me family names—Sweet Bird, Pipe Woman, and Clouding Woman—and taught me how to relate our history, to protect our people. They told the truth, but did not overburden me with the tragedy of our history. Mom would tell me to "always remember that most of the time our ancestors were visiting, singing, enjoying life—it was only sad for a short time." They also emphasized the grand blessings of being part of our family and our people.

My father, Freeland Douglas, was Muscogee; my mother, Susie Eades, was Cheyenne and Pawnee. Both were brought up in a balanced way in matrilineal traditions. Two original instructions for the Cheyenne are (1) the Nation shall be strong so long as the hearts of the women are not on the ground, and (2) the truth can come from anyone, so listen to even the smallest voice. Both Muscogee and Cheyenne cultures have functional leadership traditions. It means that, when you are a leader, you lead, but it is temporary, linked with your function. The next day you can have a follower position, so you use your power and skill to be a good follower, supportive of another's leadership. In that way, power is a shared burden, decentralized—the representative democracy that inspired the American founders and governance form. If you stay a very long time in a position of power, as they often do on Capitol Hill, it usually means you have outlasted your effectiveness and judgment.

JR: What are the important events—personal or professional—that have been instrumental in your career and in your life?

SH: I would like to start by acknowledging important events involving my ancestors that happened before my lifetime—the murder of Chief Lean Bear and the Sand Creek Massacre; the Battles of Little Bighorn and Palo Duro Canyon. In the Cheyenne language, we have no past tense. Only Is and Is Coming. It means that what has happened in the past is still present in your consciousness and in your life. The Muscogee have known the Battle of Horseshoe Bend and the Trail of Tears. These still are on our minds. Things that happened before my lifetime actually are happening to me. My parents, grandparents, and great-grandparents were beaten up in federal boarding schools for speaking their heritage languages. But they managed to keep them and pass them on. My father spoke eleven languages. During World War II, he was in the Thunderbird Division's Company C, which was comprised solely of Indian boys from Chilocco Indian School. On the troop ship to North Africa, they made up a code, based on the coordinates of Chilocco and the Muscogee languages (Seminole, Choctaw, Chickasaw, etc.) and Cherokee, Apache, and other languages of students at Chilocco. These code talkers helped win a lot of victories. Dad was wounded at Monte Cassino and ended up in a recovery hospital in Libya.

My father had a very hectic and difficult childhood. He used to run away from school and he was often chased by the bounty hunters who were paid five dollars for each runaway Native child they captured. My mother was horribly abused and didn't want to talk about it. I was brought up partly by my parents, partly by my grandparents and aunts and uncles. I had two brothers, twins, who were born when I was five. Now, only one brother and I remain, but we have children and grandchildren.

After the war, Dad finished high school at Chilocco and returned to the army, which educated him as a cryptographer and in three dialects of Chinese and Korean and other languages. We got to live in Hawaii and Italy. I was eleven when we moved to Posillipo, one of two hills in Naples. We had a wonderful view of the bay and Vesuvius. We went on trips in European and the Middle Eastern countries. We were lucky enough to go to Carrara, where Michelangelo worked with the white sparkly marble mined there. It was wonderful meeting and learning about different cultures and it was liberating not being easily identified.

I was homesick, but I didn't miss being beat up in Oklahoma for being Indian. I had wonderful teachers in Italy, especially Sra. DiGiovani, who taught music—we co-wrote the school song—and Ms. Bell, who taught English using Shakespeare. She had a Texas accent, wore cowboy boots, and made Shakespearean plays and sonnets part of our lives, language, and dreams. I remember those excellent teachers most fondly.

JR: You have been very active in the Indian Movement of 1960–1980. What—according to you—have been the most important events of that period and who are the leaders of that movement that you most admire?

SH: Our cultural rights movement formalized in 1967 at a gathering of Cheyenne, Arapaho, Lakota, and other people at our holy mountain, Bear Butte. Our coalition led directly to the efforts to protect sacred places, to reclaim our dead relatives and cultural items from museums, and to establish an Indian cultural center in front of the U.S. Capitol, so policymakers would have to look us in the face when they made laws about us.

We achieved the American Indian Religious Freedom Act (1978), the National Museum of the American Indian (1989), the Native American Graves Protection and Repatriation Act (1990), and other laws to revitalize Native languages and return lands. During the same time, there were fish-ins by Northwest tribes who successfully defended their traditional and treaty rights to catch fish on their ancestral land. We all envisioned and worked toward the time when discrimination against us would end and respect for us would begin. We've come far and made many gains, but we still have a lot of work to do.

I've had the privilege of working with myriad Native heroes. Clyde Warrior (Ponca), who founded the National Indian Youth Council in 1961 as an intertribal organization in which young Indians could promote their ideas on several fronts: voting, getting rid of ridiculous so-called Indian sports mascots, better healthcare, education, and students' rights. Vine Deloria Jr. (Standing Rock Sioux), a writer, attorney, educator, and activist, who was my political partner in so much Indian rights work. Maiselle McCloud Bridges (Puyallup/Squaxin Island), the matriarch of Franks Landing Indian Community, which was the heart of the treaty fishing rights struggle. Lucy Covington (Colville), who defeated federal termination of the Confederated Tribes of the Colville Reservation.

My husband, Frank Ray Harjo (Muscogee), was a hero. He was an activist and artist, and spent some time occupying Alcatraz Island in 1969, when we lived in New York City and produced and reported for WBAI-FM Radio Station. His father was from Oklahoma and his mother was a refugee from the Warsaw Ghetto. His parents split up and he was raised by his aunts in Okmulgee. He spoke Muscogee and English; after his mother took him to the Bronx at thirteen, he learned Hebrew for his Bar Mitzvah.

He lived in New York City and then at Onondaga Nation, near Syracuse. I often went to Onondaga for Strawberry and Mid-Winter ceremonies. We were married in a traditional Muscogee ceremony in 1971 by my Dad's relative, Phillip Deere, who was a leader of the Nuyakv Grounds. I have two children—a daughter, 44, and a son, 36. My husband died in 1982, when he was thirty-five. I would like to get more information about his mother, Frances Licht, to find out how she escaped from the Warsaw Ghetto and ended up in New York City. When she and Duke Ray Harjo lived in Oklahoma, Indians and Jews were the peoples most discriminated against. Their life was very difficult.

JR: What have been, according to you, the most important developments in the Native American field over the last twenty years?

SH: Some of the most important developments were brought about by intertribal cooperation through the National Congress of American Indians (NCAI). During the 1980s, I was NCAI executive director and had the privilege of spearheading national campaigns for repatriation, language protection, and museum reform; we also fought for treaty fishing rights and against anti-treaty hate groups in the Great Lakes area, and upheld tribal sovereignty in gaming legislation. It was a glorious time for Indian rights.

Vine Deloria Jr. brought me onto the reform board of the Museum of the American Indian in New York in 1980, and we worked with the Kiowa writer, N. Scott Momaday, and others to salvage the one million objects of the Heye collection. When I became NCAI executive director, I married our long-standing objectives of repatriation and a national museum (the cultural center we envisioned in 1967) with the goal of protecting the Museum of the American Indian collection from further deterioration.

Another board member, Charles Simon, of Solomon Brothers, said we needed a "bidding war" between New York and Washington, which were disinterested in our goals at that time. Charlie said Ross Perrot, the conservative politician, wanted a world-class museum in Texas, wasn't particular about the type, and was the very person who could make a bid and start a war.

As soon as the *New York Times* broke the news, politicians in New York and Washington started fighting over the collection. That was the beginning of the negotiations that resulted in nationalizing the collection in the Smithsonian, mandating a national repatriation policy and building an NMAI with a permanent exhibit space in New York, a cultural research facility in Maryland, and the NMAI Museum on the Mall, where it and the Capitol face each other. We won everything we envisioned at Bear Butte, and it only took us twenty-two years to do it.

But, at the beginning, I deplored the fact that not enough of the employees were Native and that it was not showing the work of contemporary living artists. The major shows in the Museum on the Mall only went to artists who were dead. Allan Houser, George Morrison, and Fritz Scholder were friends of mine and I love them and their work. They would be the first to say that the living artists deserve major exhibits, too. It is good to know that the NMAI has progressively changed its hiring and exhibition practices.

JR: What are your current projects?

SH: Of all the work we started in 1967, sacred places protection is the one we haven't finished. I'm proud to have worked on the Barack Obama presidential campaign and as an advisor to the Obama-Biden transition. During the campaign, candidate Obama promised to support legal protections for sacred places. I trust he will keep his word and, if anyone can convince Congress to establish a sacred places right of action, it is President Obama. I'm focusing on federal and state administrative protections for those sacred places under the most immediate threat, as well as the legal fix.

I'm the Harjo of *Harjo et al. v. Pro Football, Inc.* Our lawsuit against the disparaging name of the Washington professional football club is now in its seventeenth year of litigation. There are two identical cases behind us brought by young Native American people. When the first so-called Indian mascot was changed in 1970, there were more than three thousand of these Native references in American sports. Today, there are only nine hundred. So, we've eliminated two-thirds of these offenses and that's a societal sea change. We may not win our suit, but we have grandchildren and great-grandchildren, so we are well prepared to retire the remaining one-third.

I've always been too busy making history to write about it as much as I'd like to, and I'm trying to change that now and publish more. I am working on a book of my poetry and contributions to several books, including my mother's grandfather's unpublished manuscript. I'm also doing a photo book with captions for my grandson, and writing essays about work I've done, so coming generations might understand why I did what and how.

I'm guest-curating a treaties exhibit for NMAI and editing a publication for it. How I wish that we had more statements from our Native treaty-signers, including my own great-great-grandfather, Cheyenne Chief Bull Bear, about why and how they did what they did, and what they thought of it later. It makes me ever more committed to leaving a record and documenting our own time, as well as revisiting our distant history.

NATIONAL SACRED PLACES PRAYER

On ceremonies held across the country from June 19 through June 23 to mark the 2009 National Days of Prayer to Protect Native American Sacred Places.

"Native and non-Native people nationwide gather at this time for Solstice ceremonies and to honor sacred places, with a special emphasis on the need for Congress to build a door to the courts for Native nations to protect our traditional churches," said Suzan Shown Harjo (Cheyenne and Hodulgee Muscogee). She is president of the Morning Star Institute, which organizes the National Sacred Places Prayer Days.

"Many Native American sacred places are being damaged because Native nations do not have equal access under the First Amendment to defend them," said Ms. Harjo. "All other peoples in the United States can use the First Amendment to protect their churches, but the Supreme Court closed that door to Native Americans in 1988. Today, Native Americans are the only peoples in the United States who do not have a constitutional right of action to protect sacred places. That simply must change as a matter of fairness and equity. Native nations have been cobbling together protections based on defenses intended for other purposes. Those may permit lawsuits, but they do not provide a place at the table when development is being contemplated, and the Supreme Court does not appear inclined to hear lawsuits which lack a tailor-made cause of action."

During his presidential campaign in 2008, Senator Barack Obama addressed this issue as part of his Native American policy platform for religious freedom, cultural rights, and sacred places protection: "Native American sacred places and site-specific ceremonies are under threat from development, pollution, and vandalism. Barack Obama supports legal protections for sacred places and cultural traditions, including Native ancestors' burial grounds and churches."

"Native Americans were heartened by this statement and look forward to President Obama fulfilling his promise," said Ms. Harjo . . .

—News Statement, Morning Star Institute

Richard West, lawyer and founding director of the National Museum of the American Indian

The first director of the National Museum of the American Indian (NMAI), Richard West (Southern Cheyenne) has forged new concepts and achieved many goals that seemed totally unrealistic to most non-Indians and many Indians before the opening of the NMAI. His education in an artistic family and his legal training were combined to lead the way toward understanding and reconciliation in the field of Native art and Native heritage.

This interview took place in Paris, where he was attending a UNESCO meeting for the International Council of Museums (ICOM) and was getting ready to retire, in September 2007. Since then he has been replaced by another lawyer, Kevin Gover (Pawnee and Shoshone), former U.S. Interior Assistant Secretary of Indian Affairs.

West directed the NMAI for seventeen years (1990–2007). He was active both on the national and the international scene. He played an instrumental role, as a "man between two worlds," an ambassador of Native culture in the United States and abroad. In this interview he explains the genesis of the museum foundation. Looking back he is pleased to have contributed to creating: a "safe place for unsafe ideas."[1]

Joëlle Rostkowski: As director of the National Museum of the American Indian, which opened its doors in September 2004, and looking back on its opening and its activities since then, how could you describe its main characteristics and achievements?

Richard West: I consider that, on the whole, what we see today is what we had in view. The museum has been a collective undertaking; it emerged from a set of ideas debated by the Board of Trustees. Personally, being a lawyer and not a museum expert, I knew that we needed some consultations, but I also felt that we had to conceive something new, really different. I wanted to listen to informed people and to ask the communities themselves how they wanted to be represented.

Richard West *(Courtesy of the National Museum of the American Indian [NMAI])*

I grew up in an artistic family, Indian (Cheyenne) on my father's side and non-Indian on my mother's side. My father was a painter and sculptor and my mother a pianist. I grew up around museums and I knew how difficult it was for artists—and particularly Indian artists—to be recognized.

Initially I started with two main ideas: First I wanted the museum to represent the full spectrum of Indigenous peoples. Second, I thought that we had to invoke Native voices and integrate those voices into the presentation of the collections.

That was the foundation of the new objectives we set for the museum. We conceived a museum that was to become not only a cultural space but also a community center. To the consternation of some people it has asserted its difference, its specificity as a civic space where one is confronted not only with Native objects but also with the native experience.

However the museum is not designed for Native peoples only. It is conceived as a place for dialogue; it is supposed to enhance mutual understanding and respect. As far as the programming around exhibitions is concerned, non-Natives have also been involved. We have been engaged in "dialogical conversations," joined symposia. And some Native artists have exhibited at the Venice Festival. James Luna, for example, and Edgar Heap of Birds have put together installations, have represented their own visions at the Biennale. And that's so much better than the marginalized position in which Native artists—and I think of my own father—have been confined for so many years. Artists in those days were drawn into a corner by mainstream society and—simultaneously—they were criticized by their own communities if they succeeded in the outside world.

JR: The National Museum of the American Indian owns a considerable collection of Native objects numbering almost one million pieces, all coming from the Heye collection, located for many years in New York. George Heye was a very eager collector of Native artifacts but not particularly interested in Native experience. How do you relate to the Heye collection?

RW: I went to see the Heye collection in New York when I was a teenager. I remember I was thirteen and I admired their fine collection of Cheyenne items. George Heye was the most important collector of his time, the collector of an era. He was willing to salvage those artifacts; his ambition as a collector led him to launch a cultural salvage operation. I don't know whether he cared about the people. His concern about Indian communities remains open to question.

I remember seeing a Pomo basket-maker from California who discovered the Heye collection of fine baskets from her community. She burst into tears. She said how sad she was the baskets were there and—at the same time—how fortunate it was that they had been kept and cared for at the museum.

At the NMAI, we have both deconstructed Heye's vision and reconstructed it. I don't know what he would think of what we have done. We have been trying to reconnect Native Americans with the whole collection, because it's part of everybody's heritage in Native America. It gives Indian communities a feeling of pride.

JR: Could you comment upon the treatment of objects at the NMAI? Is there anything specific, different from practices in other museums?

RW: We do have a respectful approach to artifacts. We consider that objects have a life of their own, a power related to their history and the rituals they have been associated with. We think that Native communities should be involved in the treatment of artifacts. The different tribes are consulted on what kind of objects should be put on display and how they should be handled.

The notion of *cultural care* is very important. Curators are aware of some important principles concerning the directions in which the objects should be placed, what should be put next to them. They are supposed to respect the rules relating to gender and have a sense of the sacred. For example the sacred pipes are considered so powerful—their spiritual power is so strong—that when they are put on display in the museum the bowl and the stem are separated. They are reunited only for ceremonial use.

The sacredness of objects is very important. I know from my own experience that some objects that have been used in certain circumstances have a special value and are endowed with a certain power. Sometimes a healing power. When I was recovering from surgery, I was wearing a blanket used by my brother during a Cheyenne sun dance. It was an object that had been prayed over; it was a comfort to me and it gave me strength.

Objects tell a story. They have a language. To interpret the objects, you need to know the history of the communities and the meaning of the ceremonies. They sometimes have a spiritual dimension that exceeds their aesthetic value.

We do have a sense of aesthetics about the objects but we should also realize that artifacts tell us something. They become a platform for conversations, they bring about an awareness, and they support a narrative. A museum is not only a palace of collections. In the case of the NMAI, it should also be a showcase for Indigenous values and creativity.

JR: How do you view the objections of some anthropologists who have criticized the NMAI for lacking anthropological and historical background and scholarship?

RW: In our permanent exhibitions, such as *Our Peoples*, we have tried to give voice to our histories. It means that American Indians tell their own histories. History becomes a collection of subjective tellings by many different voices. In the permanent exhibitions called *Our Universes*, we focus on Native cosmology and ancestral Native teachings. In *Our Lives* we deal with contemporary life and identities. I know that a number of historians and a few old-fashioned anthropologists have objected to that approach. Actually I respect anthropologists and greatly admire some of them, for example Claude Lévi-Strauss who has so brilliantly interpreted Native cultures and shown a remarkable insight into cultural essence.

In the NMAI we have created a "museum different." We have given a voice to people who have been neglected for too long, including small groups. Twenty-four different communities are represented. Twelve from the United States, four from Canada, and eight from Central and South America. We have insisted on presenting some small groups such as the Powhatan, Piscataway from Washington, D.C., and also urban Indians who have long been ignored by museums. The objects exhibited were selected by the people themselves.

Actually what we have is a museum in three sites. Three facilities are part of the NMAI: The George Gustav Heye Center, which opened in the historic Alexander Hamilton House Custom House in lower Manhattan in 1994, organizes exhibitions and reminds the visitors of New York's historical association with the Heye collection. The second building, the Cultural Resources Center, was completed in 1998 in Washington's Maryland suburbs. It is a conservation and storage facility. But it is also much more than that; it is where objects are taken care of. It is a home to the collections and it is also a place for research and scholarship. The third building is our spectacular museum built on the National Mall, according to the original design of Douglas Cardinal (Blackfoot) and a team of Native designers.

I always considered that the museum's architecture was supposed to be well adapted to the mission of the institution, to the presentation of the objects and the representation of Native cultures. It's not a museum for curators. It's what I call a safe place for unsafe ideas. We have conceived it as a place where Native voices can be heard, as a forum where Native peoples can interpret their cultural inheritance and contemporary lives.

I consider that museums should foster debate, confrontations, lead to discourse dialogue, and interactivity, important engagements. They should be intellectually vibrant. Visiting a museum should not be a passive experience.

From the very beginning of the opening of the museum, we have put together temporary exhibits of contemporary artists. We started with Allan Houser, Apache sculptor, and the Chippewa painter Bill Morrison. Then we had a retrospective of the painter Fritz Scholder, who died in 2005.

Generally speaking we are working on second-generation exhibits; they will complete the permanent exhibitions. And give new insights on Native arts and cultures.

JR: Would you say, to sum up the importance of your role at the head of the museum, that you have been trying to break new ground in the museum field?

RW: I hope that breaking new ground could be considered as part of my legacy. I am going to retire because I believe I have done the work I had in mind.

I believe in cycles and I feel a new cycle in my life will be starting soon. I am very active on the international scene, within ICOM in particular, and I am eager to continue in that direction.

To come back to my legacy as founding director of NMAI, I have been trying, with a very committed team of enthusiastic collaborators, to raise significant questions, to engage in debates on the historical role of museums, to raise questions that should continue to be discussed in the years to come. My personal background has been to cross borders. I have always lived along the borderlands of two worlds. When I conceived the museum, with the assistance and contribution of many others, I always asked myself not only how Native peoples should represent themselves but also whether the larger culture would be willing to accept those representations.

And I decided that we could try to create a museum that would foster respect and reconciliation.

MEDIATION

Becoming Mediators of the Law

Shortly before I assumed the directorship of the Museum, the Congress of the United States passed the Native American Graves Protection Act of 1990, a federal statute mandating the return, upon application from Native communities and after legal process, of certain parts of Native collections that sit in a number of America's major museums. The returns were to be made to Native communities culturally affiliated with certain kinds of collections in museums and included human remains, funerary materials, and sacred and ceremonial objects . . .

When I first became the director, an issue still lingering from the Museum's predecessor institution, the Heye Foundation Museum of the American Indian in New York, concerned the return of potlatch materials from the Cape Mudge and Alert Bay communities in Canada. The questions were several (including the Museum's obligation to make cross-international boundary repatriations), but the first was whether, since the materials had be confiscated "legally," under a then-extant Canadian law prohibiting potlatch ceremonies, the Museum was under any "legal" obligation to repatriate at all. The Museum determined, ultimately, that whatever the purely legal analytics, it had an ethical obligation to return the material since the Canadian law under which the material originally was seized had long been repealed.

A second example serves to make the same general point. Among the Museum's more complicated repatriations have been those involving multiple claimants to material where the trail of cultural affiliation or provenance information is less than completely revealing. In two cases to date and each involving several different Native communities, the Museum's Office of Repatriation has faced a situation where the legal mandates and structure of the repatriation legislation and, even the invocation of ethical perspectives, are beside the main point.

The initial impulse of the repatriation applicants was a gesture to the Museum that basically said, "You decide"—an invitation intentionally declined by the institution since the underpinning principle of the American repatriation schema is community authority. In this case the Museum's Office of Repatriation served as "convener" and "mediator," while the applicants, not always comfortably but finally successfully, retained the rightful role of decision-maker.

In the past two decades, repatriation movements in the United States, Canada, New Zealand, and Australia have definitively redressed relationships between Indigenous peoples and the museums holding their cultural patrimony. The establishment of this framework of cultural property rights, however, is but the first, if perhaps the most important and seminal, step in a far longer journey. Through the course of that journey, the capacity of museums, and for that matter, Native communities themselves, to utilize imagination and flexibility—and indeed, mediation in many instances—will enhance and facilitate more rapid progress in all quarters.

—Richard West, Jr.
International Council of Museums (ICOM)
ICOM News No. 3, 2006

CHAPTER FOUR

Emil Her Many Horses, curator, National Museum of the American Indian

Emil Her Many Horses (Oglala Lakota) is a member of the Oglala Lakota tribe and an accomplished beadwork artist, winner of the 2001 Best of Show category for his tribute to the Lakota Sioux Vietnam Veterans at the Northern Plains Tribal Arts Show. He is a curator of many talents, who has studied theology and is very interested in philosophy.

After becoming director of the Buechel Memorial Lakota Museum on the Rosebud Reservation in South Dakota, where he started an outstanding collection of quilts made by Lakota women, he would later be hired by the National Museum of the American Indian (NMAI). He was lead curator for one of the three inaugural permanent exhibitions titled: *Our Universes: Indigenous Philosophies and Cosmologies*. In 2007, as a permanent curator at the NMAI, he organized and coordinated one of the most successful exhibitions of the new museum: *Identity by Design: Tradition, Change and Celebration in Native Women's Dresses.*

This interview took place in 2008 at the NMAI, as he was working on a new exhibition titled: *A Song for the Horse Nation.*

Joëlle Rostkowski: You were born and raised on South Dakota reservations and you work and live in Washington, D.C., where you have become a permanent curator at the NMAI. Do you perceive yourself as a Lakota Indian or rather as a curator specialized in Plains Indian cultures?

Emil Her Many Horses: I am an enrolled member of the Oglala Lakota tribe from Pine Ridge, South Dakota. This is where my parents lived and worked. My father was working for the Public Health Service and he eventually transferred and moved the family to Sicangu Lakota reservation at Rosebud, South Dakota.

Emil Her Many Horses *(Photo by Nicolas Rostkowski)*

I call both Rosebud and Pine Ridge my home. Rosebud is where I attended school. We have eight children in our family. My parents instilled in us the importance of getting a good education. Six of us have received a BA degree and one has received her master's degree. My parents would eventually go back to school; my mother received an AA degree in nursing, and after my father retired he went back to school. He posthumously received his BA in education two months after his death.

My sister Grace is an accomplished shawl dancer, received her degree in criminal justice, and has recently accepted a position on the Rosebud as the head of their law enforcement department. Cleve, one of my younger brothers, serves as the Bureau of Indian Affairs superintendant on the Rosebud. I have personally been through a very long and diversified educational process.

I received my Bachelor of Arts in business administration from Augustana College in Sioux Falls, South Dakota. After graduation I was a bank manager trainee for about a year. I then returned to Rosebud where I took a position in the business office at Sinte Gleska College. My next position would be as the accounting supervisor for the St. Francis Indian Mission, a Jesuit-run mission on the reservation. Associated with the mission was a small museum called the Buechel Memorial Lakota Museum. I would eventually be the director of this museum.

As I worked with the Jesuits, I became very interested in their order, which I would eventually enter. I left home and spent seven years in Jesuit formation, first at the novitiate in St. Paul, Minnesota where I took my first vows. I would do two years of philosophy studies and first-year theology studies at Loyola University in Chicago, Illinois.

Throughout this period I still had a strong interest in Native cultures, particularly material culture. I continued to follow the efforts of the National Museum of the American Indian to build a museum.

The decision to return to the museum field was a great internal struggle for me. I wondered what would be the best decision for me to follow. I went to a retreat house to pray about it. With the blessing of my formation director, I would spend a year in researching collections of NMAI in New York and finally decided to leave the Jesuits and to go back to the museum field.

After my year of research ended and I decided to leave the Jesuits, I planned on returning to graduate museum studies. Bruce Bernstein, director of NMAI's Cultural Resources Center, asked if I would be interested in joining the curatorial staff and helping with inaugural exhibitions. I became the lead curator for the exhibition titled *Our Universes* with the focus on traditional philosophies.

JR: You had the opportunity to be involved in one of the most revolutionary museum projects in the history of the United States. The National Museum of the American Indian was built by a Native architect, Douglas Cardinal, and most members of its staff are Natives. Its philosophy is very different from an ethnographic museum.

EHMH: The NMAI initiated a new approach to Native museums. Initially, when I started getting involved in the preparatory work, the curatorial staff was located in New York City and eventually the staff and entire collection would be moved to a new facility in Suitland, Maryland. For five years, I traveled and established contacts with Native communities that were selected for inclusion in the *Our Universes* exhibition. The idea was to give communities a voice. The communities would have the final approval of their exhibitions in philosophies, histories, and identities. For the three inaugural exhibitions we worked in teams: curators, project managers, researchers, photographers, and media departments. We traveled throughout the whole Western hemisphere; we selected communities from the Far North in Alaska and from North America, Central America, and South America.

It was both very interesting and difficult to experiment with new concepts to try to present an internal community voice to the exhibition. And, when it was over, as we were getting ready for the opening, we didn't know what to expect from the visitors. We literally had been breaking new ground. And when the exhibitions were completed and the museum ready to be opened, we brought our community curators from many different communities to Washington. I still remember that when our Mapuche community curators from Chile saw their exhibition in the museum they cried and hugged and thanked me.

We had to face a number of technical difficulties: the architecture, with its beautiful curves, was a challenge to our designers. We had to deal with the curved walls in our space. We also had major priorities, including the transmission of traditional knowledge. Native spiritual beliefs and values live in traditional knowledge, which is passed from one generation to the next. This is why, in the museum, the visitors have the opportunity to listen to and read the quotes from our Native community curators.

In the section *Our Universes*, we stressed Native philosophies, Indigenous cosmologies, traditional ways of explaining the creation and order of the universe. Our traditions and our philosophies of life come from our elders. They taught us to live in harmony with all forms of life: plants, animals, and humans; to be aware of the spirit world around us. They have kept our collective memory alive through ceremonies, celebrations, and through a certain wisdom expressed in daily life.

JR: *Identity by Design,* the exhibition that you conceived and co-curated with Colleen Cutschall, was praised by Richard West, then-director of the NMAI, as a great success. What was the genesis of that exhibit?

EHMH: Looking back, I remember that I was in Santa Fe, at the Institute of American Indian Arts (IAIA), during Indian Market. It was in 2005, I was listening to Scott Momaday recite a memory of a Kiowa woman from his tribe—she had been buried in her finest buckskin dress, decorated with elk's teeth. It made me reflect on that powerful image and reminded me of the stories I had been told by my own grandmothers. Memories of these women and their dresses still remain with me. I started thinking about a dress exhibit and put forth a proposal. I thought it was important to listen to women's voices, to stress their courage and creativity.

The proposal went back and forth for a year. It took a while to define the exact scope and significance of the show. Should we exhibit dresses from all over the whole continent? I thought it would be too much. Finally it was decided to concentrate on the Plains, Plateau, and Great Basin regions, from the 1800s to the present. The idea was to present the evolution of women's dress and demonstrate its strong significance for Native people.

Material culture is very revealing of the succession of historical events. We wanted to put in evidence, not only the artistry and the variety of styles, but also the stories that can be told about women's lives and their role in their community. Adornments have changed over the years, whenever new materials were introduced by English, French, Russian, and Spanish traders. Respect for tradition doesn't mean that styles have been static. My priority was to show how Native artists incorporate new materials in their dresses while remaining faithful to traditional identities.

JR: In the book entitled *Identity by Design* that you co-edited for the exhibition, it is mentioned that elaborate beading has been, especially among the Lakota, a defiant response to social disruption and the threat of assimilation at the end of the nineteenth century.

EHMH: The end of the reservation era was a time of tremendous social pressure. It was believed that Indians in reservations—in particular Indian women—would give up their artistic traditions. But actually the cultural significance of traditional dress has remained very strong.

Techniques have been passed down by generations of Native women, even during the wars and in reservations. Styles have evolved over the years as new materials and influences are adapted in the clothing design. Women artists maintained tribal distinctions in their artwork. They took advantage of the extra time available once they were confined to reservations. These women artists accomplished elaborate works such as dresses, cradles, moccasins, and leggings. They found innovative ways to blend the old with the new. They were proving that they could survive, materially and spiritually.

I think that this exhibition has been considered as a success because it demonstrates that dress is a complex expression of culture and identity. At the NMAI in Washington we are fortunate to work with a talented staff, and we had sufficient space to display both fronts and backs of the dresses. The result was spectacular. We even managed to include dresses from the time of the Ghost Dance movement from 1890, which today are rarely exhibited. We obtained permission from community spiritual leaders to display these dresses.

A year later, in 2008, the same exhibition was reassembled in our New York facility. I was very concerned about the space needed for the displays but all went well. The show was well received in New York City. Our Native dresses were the high fashion of their day and to us can equal any of the fashions featured in this center of vibrant culture.

JR: What are the new projects you are working on now?

EHMH: Currently, I have opened our newest exhibition titled *A Song for the Horse Nation*. The exhibition features the impact of the horse on Native cultures particularly in the Northern Hemisphere. The horse has been a strong component of Plains culture and the NMAI has a great collection of horse gear and other objects associated with the horse, such as horse masks, saddles, bridles, *ledger* art, and clothing depicting horse imagery.

Horses were important in community life and in social relationships. By raiding enemy horses a young man could prove his bravery. In Native cultures generosity is considered an important quality and giving horses away at naming ceremonies and at memorial ceremonies reflects the generosity of the owner. Receiving a beautiful horse is considered a great honor. Many contemporary artists are still inspired by the image of the horse through our stories, songs, and artwork. All these elements have been taken into account to prepare this exhibition, entitled *A Song for a Horse Nation*, and the related book, co-edited with George Horse Capture.

JR: Looking back to what you have achieved, do you feel that you have made the right choices? Now that you are a permanent curator in a major national museum, do you feel that you have accomplished your childhood dreams?

EHMH: I think I have made the right choices. I chose to take advantage of my traditional knowledge to contribute to a better understanding of Native culture. I have chosen Native art. It's both a privilege and a constant challenge to be working as a curator at the NMAI in Washington. I feel I have exceeded many of my childhood dreams.

IDENTITY BY DESIGN

Each dress holds a story. Most dresses in museum collections have documentation about who collected the dress, but little is known about who made the dress. Rarely do we know much about the rich spirit and thought involved in its creation. With living dressmakers, we are fortunate to be able to gain insight into this process. Listen, for example, to the words of Juanita Growing Thunder Fogarty: "A lot of dresses have sound. I have coins on my dress. I like it when I can hear the clinking of coins or the snapping of my fringes when I'm dancing. It's all part of the feeling that the dress is alive." And Jackie Parsons, our dress designer and an artist from the Blackfeet Nation of Montana, encompasses much as she says, "When I'm wearing a Blackfeet dress that I have made, I feel really powerful, because I feel so very connected to everything around me."

The beautiful dresses in *Identity by Design*—made by women from Native nations on both sides of the U.S./Canada border—reveal the artistic talent and individuality of their creators as well as different regional styles and tribal designs. Ranging in time from the 1830s to the present day, they serve to illuminate Native history and identity during a time of intense social and cultural change. For contemporary women artists, dresses are more than garments. They are evidence of a proud and unbroken tradition, links to the generations of women who came before them, and bridges to the future.

—Emil Her Many Horses
"Portraits of Native Women and Their Dresses,"
in *Identity by Design*, National Museum of the American Indian,
Smithsonian Institution (New York: Harper Collins, 2007)

CHAPTER FIVE

Sven Haakanson, director of the Alutiiq Museum, Kodiak, Alaska

Sven Haakanson (Sugpiaq) is executive director of the Alutiiq Museum of Kodiak, Alaska. He is also a skilled carver and talented photographer. A Native Alaskan with training in archeology and anthropology, he has been instrumental in the cultural revival of his community. Shortly after earning his PhD from Harvard University, he accepted the position of director in the new community museum.[1]

The Alutiiq Museum grew from the Kodiak Native Association's Culture and Heritage program (KANA) dedicated to promoting awareness of Alutiiq history, language, and arts. In 1993 KANA received a $1.5 million grant from the EXXON Valdez Oil Spill Trustee Council. The Alutiiq Museum and Archeological Repository opened its door in May 1995.

Over the past decade Native-run institutions in the Alaskan Gulf Coast have developed ways and means to rediscover, preserve, and promote their cultural heritage. The Alutiiq Museum is one such institution as it has defined itself as a repository of archeological, ethnological, and archival material. It also supports research on culture and history and language revitalization.

Sven Haakanson has been a driving force behind the most impressive accomplishments of the new museum. He has led a large-scale study of sacred Alutiiq sites to identify and document petroglyphs and stone carvings. He has organized traveling exhibits of antiquities to museums in Alaska and established contacts with other significant collections of Sugpiaq art in Russia, France, and Germany.

This interview focuses on a unique experience of exchange and cooperation made possible by sharing of knowledge and the development of goodwill on both sides of the Atlantic. Communication and cooperation between the Alutiiq Museum of Kodiak and the Château-Musée de Boulogne-sur-Mer, has led to the exhibition in

Sven Haakanson *(Courtesy of the Kodiak Museum)*

Kodiak of a unique collection of Alutiiq masks collected by the French explorer and anthropologist Alphonse Pinart.

Pinart, a native of Boulogne-sur-Mer, donated his extensive and impressive collection of masks to the city. The masks were hidden and preserved during the bombings of the Second World War and they are now reinterpreted with the precious knowledge of the Alutiiq Museum team, the cooperation of Kodiak elders, and Native artists inspired by the tradition of mask carvings.

Joëlle Rostkowski: At a very early age—in your mid-thirties—after finishing your PhD dissertation, you had the opportunity to become the director of a new museum, located on your native soil. You have been a brilliant student and you are an artist and photographer. How did you react when you received that job proposal?

Sven Haakanson: As a Native I never felt that I would have had such an opportunity in my life. However, very early on the elders made me aware of the importance of our cultural knowledge, language, memory, and of cultural preservation. My grandmother, who grew up at the very place where Pinart collected some of these masks and all the songs after he arrived in Kodiak, had always spoken to me in Alutiiq. She was unique because to speak in our language was forbidden by the school teachers, and my parents, like all others, were forced not to pass on our language. There was a stigma attached to speaking your native tongue.

I went to the local school in Old Harbor and my last two years in Anchorage, then to the University of Alaska (Fairbanks) and eventually left for the East Coast, to Harvard University, where I received my PhD in anthropology with a focus in archaeology. I chose a degree that would lead me back to my roots. Studying archaeology and anthropology, I wished to be able to serve in an institution related to my Native culture.

I spent several years in Siberia, Russia, where I had the honor to work with Native peoples who lived traditionally. I was struck by the fact that they had managed to preserve much of their traditions, in spite of colonization. Having been under the domination of Russia for five hundred years, it seemed to me that they had not lost as much as we have in two hundred years.

So, when I was offered the opportunity to become the director of our new museum, I thought I was given the chance of a lifetime to accomplish something out of a dream while at the same time serving my community as my father had instilled in me to do. My PhD was not completed then and I accepted the job only after obtaining my degree.

JR: As a director of the Alutiiq Museum you have proved very good at establishing collaborative relationships with museums throughout the world. You seem to have a special ability to bridge cultures and continents.

SH: I am myself of mixed ancestry and have traveled and been exposed to many other cultures. But I think it's more a question of attitude and depends on the determination to concentrate on positive exchanges. I have always felt that it was important to develop human-to-human exchanges, to give the example of crossing boundaries.

Our history has been dramatic but, when I look at European history, I realize that so many countries have had to face war on their land, bombings on their cities, and destruction of their cultural heritage. I do think that we have to connect people through stories, through art, through exchanges.

Being director of a museum offers many opportunities to engage in uplifting projects. Museums are not mausoleums and they should become and be a living part of our communities. This is why in Kodiak, at our museum, we have a Community Archaeology program, we teach our language, and we offer carving workshops. We want our museum to be more than a repository. We encourage and work with artisans, students, and scholars. Being a carver and a photographer myself, I know how important it is to make things, to transmit knowledge through the actual objects, through gestures, through active participation, through the sharing of knowledge by getting each person to create each piece. This experience links them to our history in ways only creating can—one on one and hands on.

At the Alutiiq Museum we have a team of twelve people who are very dedicated. Some are locally trained, others are university graduates. With twelve staff members we have managed to involve the community, to organize programs like our traveling arts workshops for children and to welcome foreign visitors.

I also have traveled extensively to document and identify Sugpiaq artifacts. The partnership between Alutiiq Museum and the Museum (Château-Musée) of Boulogne-sur-Mer for the Sugpiaq mask exhibit has been extremely fruitful and stimulating for both parties.

JR: Masks have had a major place in traditional Sugpiaq rituals. Alphonse Pinart collected his masks in the 1870s, when they were concealed from the disapproving view of colonizers. They were considered as examples of the belief in evil gods.

SH: A lot of our traditions were lost after the Russian conquest, in 1784. Pre-contact religious rituals and customs were banned and most of the local people were converted to Christianity. We became Russian Orthodox. The rule of the Russian Empire was that all the Kodiak people who were converted to Christianity became full Russian citizens.

I remember learning all the Orthodox prayers by heart in Old Church Slavonic. In the nineteenth century our traditional rituals faded and the traditional masks appeared as symbols of savagery and paganism. To many missionaries our dances and our songs were considered pagan rituals to be eradicated.

Traditionally, crafted and ornamented masks held a very important, mystical place in classical Sugpiaq culture. Through masked dancing, during winter festivals, we maintained the balance with the spirits and all the forces that controlled our daily lives. The masks represented the spirit world and the winter festival was usually held after the hunting season.

Our craftsmen gathered drift logs of yew, fir, or cedar, or harvested birch, and carved stylized masks in a variety of styles. There is a prevalence of spirit masks but some appear to have been portraits of people.

Most masked dances were accompanied by stories and songs. Those performances were part of the hunting ceremony. During the nineteenth century masked dancing progressively blended with Russian folk traditions and the calendar of performances was adapted to church holidays.

JR: Looking back at the partnership established with the Museum of Boulogne-sur-Mer, do you recall the most important steps that led you to convince the French authorities to let this unique collection of Sugpiaq masks travel back to Kodiak for the 2008 exhibition entitled *Giinaquq: Like a Face*?

SH: The Pinart mask collection is unique. This is why I felt it was very important to establish a partnership with France in that matter. The Pinart collection, with its large and well-documented assemblage of masks, provides a detailed look into the nineteenth-century Kodiak Sugpiaq artistic customs and spiritual beliefs. It's the only assemblage of its kind in the world.

Alphonse Pinart was one of the very few foreign scholars to hear Sugpiaq songs, to watch masked dances, and to attend a winter festival and systematically document this entire experience. Pinart traveled with Native people in kayaks to remote villages. While he has been called an amateur, he was actually in many ways a visionary. He was a self-trained linguist and what we would call an anthropologist today, making mention of the cultural context and the spiritual practices associated with the masks.

His research was focused on Sugpiaq ceremonial practices. Nobody knows how a young outsider could gain access to so many powerful religious songs, stories, and artifacts. He was led to some of the caves where our people kept ceremonial gear and he may have commissioned some carvings to take back to France. He remained silent about his procurement techniques, however. This still remains a mystery.

Pinart traveled to Alaska in 1871–1872, just after the transfer to American rule. Alaska had been ceded to the United States in 1867 and the villages where Pinart traveled were undergoing dramatic changes. It was a time of transition. Traditional ceremonies involving carved wooden masks had lost their prominence but were still performed on rare occasions. The objects that Pinart collected were still in use but they had been marginalized by this time.

It is only in the last two decades that Pinart's collection has attracted so much attention, after some good research done by a couple of scholars (Dr. Lydia Black and her doctoral student Dominique Desson)[2] in the early 1990s. They worked on some pieces of the Pinart collection that had been transferred from Boulogne-sur-Mer to the Musée de l'Homme du Trocadéro, in Paris, and then to the Musée du Quai Branly, the latter having inherited the Trocadéro collections.

In 2001, I began working to bring a selection of the Pinart collection's masks to Kodiak for exhibition. The new Musée du Quai Branly was not yet open but, within the framework of its future mission, it was working on an exhibition of the masks at Musée de la Porte Dorée, in Paris. The curator, Emmanuel Desveaux, invited me to write an article for the catalog on the meaning of the collection for the Kodiak people. We had discussed the possibility of bringing the masks over to Kodiak to be exhibited. However, at that time, mixed feelings about repatriation of Native objects put an end to this potential project. Fear of the consequences of the Native American Graves Protection and Repatriation Act (NAGPRA) made it difficult to obtain approval from the French authorities. It was only a few years later, after a meeting in Leuven (Belgium) organized by a scholarly group of European scholars, the American Indian Workshop, that some mediators contributed to a better understanding.

One of the scholars attending that Belgian conference, American anthropologist Sarah Froning Deleporte, who was then living in France, opened the door for a new dialogue. Having heard the frustrations we faced attempting to form a trustworthy relationship that would allow us to exhibit the masks in Alaska, she volunteered to help. She had done research on French museums,[3] had just finished doctoral study for the University of Chicago, and she could develop a project proposal that the city of Boulogne might be convinced to support. Simultaneously, the Museum of Boulogne-sur-Mer was in transition to a new leadership. The new director, Anne-Claire Laronde, was representative of a new generation willing to make the collections more accessible to the people whose heritage they reflected. She listened to the proposal and agreed to support the project.

Meanwhile, in Kodiak, we had been sharing the mask collection through photographs and we had put together an outreach program to rural villages and started mask-making workshops. Photos were an inspiration for student carvers. In addition to that, we received a grant and were able to take ten Sugpiaq carvers to France to see their ancestors' work. This trip was a turning point because a sense of trust started developing between both institutions. On both sides, people reconsidered stereotypes. French officials could overcome the fear of repatriation and Sugpiaq artists felt gratitude for the preservation of their heritage on French soil.

The deputy mayor of Boulogne-sur-Mer agreed to a loan based on this exchange. Thirty-five pieces from the French museum were sent to Kodiak (thirty-four masks and a bird-shaped feast bowl). The exhibition in Kodiak took place in May 2008, to coincide with the annual community Crab Festival celebrating its fiftieth anniversary. The *Giinaquq: Like a Face* exhibition stayed for four months at the Alutiiq Museum and then traveled to the Anchorage Museum at Rasmussen Center, where it stayed for another four months before the objects returned to France.

JR: In the catalog of the Giinaquq exhibition at the Alutiiq Museum in Kodiak, it is stressed that the exhibition was a success and drew large crowds. It also marked the success of a partnership with the Museum of Boulogne-sur-Mer. Will it lead to further exchanges and sharing of knowledge between the two institutions?

SH: During the exhibition, it was obvious that the Kodiak community was eager to rediscover its heritage. Elders came for a preview and talked about the masks. Dance groups welcomed the old masks with performances. Young people were taught mask-making and the contemporary artists who had traveled to France created and interpreted their own masks.

I believe that such a partnership between Boulogne-sur-Mer and Kodiak is a positive way to look at history. It's a win-win relationship. We have restitution of knowledge instead of mere restitution of artifacts. We observe the revitalization of traditional dances and songs, the transmission of know-how between generations.

History has been marked by a lot of suffering on both sides. And we are grateful to the team of the Museum of Boulogne-sur-Mer who allowed it to happen. Alutiiq elders and the community leaders gave their word—the masks are now back in Boulogne. It's fortunate that such a unique collection could be preserved during the two world wars.

The Kodiak people have contributed to the reinterpretation of the masks. The Museum of Boulogne-sur-Mer has put them back in their cultural context, with a new scenography and is considering another exhibition with our cooperation. Some of our Kodiak artists are planning to work and teach in Boulogne.

We have been working hard to bring back dignity and pride to our culture. We have come a long way and we have broken new ground.

WHAT ABOUT REPATRIATIONS?

. . . That was the question the French government asked. If the masks return to Alaska, will the Alaskans give them back? There is no evidence that Pinart acquired his collection under anything but honorable circumstances, however, either purchasing and trading for them, or receiving them as gifts. He had a lot of money. Also, it turns out U.S. laws governing the return of culturally important objects to Native communities apply only to American museums that receive federal funding.

At remarks given at a pre-opening reception on Friday night, Perry Eaton* applauded the cooperation between the Alaskan and French institutions. "I would have said that Alaska would get these masks loaned back to us right after the French government loaned the Winged Victory back to Greece."

Anchorage Museum director James Pepper Henry said, insofar as he could determine, this was the first time that any European museum had loaned Native American pieces to any Native American group. "Other museums in Europe are keeping an eye on this exhibit," he said.

—Mike Dunham
Anchorage Daily News, October 8, 2008

*Kodiak artist, photographer and talented mask-carver, founding president and chief executive officer of Alaska Native Heritage Center.

Perry Eaton carved a mask in honor of Alphonse Pinart. A mask burning ceremony was held at the Château-Musée (Boulogne-sur-Mer) in September 2011.

CHAPTER SIX

Veronica Tiller, historian, consultant, and writer

Veronica Tiller (Apache Jicarilla), who was a rodeo champion in her childhood, is a strong and forceful woman, whose sensitivity remains well hidden until she has established a relationship based upon mutual trust. Her research and work as a historian has always been geared toward practical aims. She enjoys doing research to bring about concrete change. Veronica is a traditional woman, who speaks her own language and who is respectful of her tribal rituals and values. She is also a modern woman living in an urban environment who has managed her own company and has conceived and supervised many projects at the tribal and intertribal levels.

Going beyond what could have remained a career focusing on the defense of Indian rights, she has also established strong ties with European universities, where she has participated in many symposiums. Lately she also has cooperated with UNESCO on a program dealing with the promotion of films on the preservation of Native lands. Recently she has decided to devote most of her time to personal research, editing, and writing.[1]

Joëlle Rostkowski: As a Native American scholar, you have been very successful in writing an evenhanded account of the history of your own community (*The Jicarilla Apache Tribe: A History [1846–1970]*). As a business consultant, you also have directed intensive research from East to West to document the contemporary social and economic conditions of all five hundred and sixty-two Indian tribes of the United States, resulting in the publication of an award-winning national reference guide: *Tiller's Guide to Indian Country*. Do you think of yourself as a Jicarilla or, in more general terms, as a Native American woman?

Veronica Tiller: I define myself as a Native American historian. When I was working on my PhD at the University of New Mexico, I wanted to write my tribal history.

Veronica Tiller *(Photo by Nicolas Rostkowski)*

This was the reason I applied to graduate school in the first place. The Velarde family is a family of chiefs and my maternal grandfather had told me many stories about my ancestors. I wanted to write about their vision, their wisdom, and their leadership. They had done a lot in establishing our reservation in Northern New Mexico in 1887 and in bringing our people together. The history of our tribe had never been written and, when I went to the Indian boarding school in Dulce, our main town, I never heard anything about our history.

Assimilation was the main objective of government boarding schools. We were considered as savages, as pagans, as late as the 1950s and early 1960s. I wanted to do something with the knowledge given to me by my grandparents and, when I went to the University of New Mexico, during the Civil Rights movement, in the 1970s, there was a surge of Native pride that encouraged me.

There was a rise in the development of Native studies at that time in many universities. I had a very nice professor, called Richard Ellis, who taught Native American history and I was inspired by his course. My undergraduate major was political science but I chose American history as my graduate subject. I received my PhD in American Indian history in 1976. The University of New Mexico (UNM) was then the only university offering such a degree. In most universities Native studies was only a minor field for students graduating in American history.

My interest and my research in history is an important part of who I am and what I wanted to do in my life. The historical perception of Native Americans, all the stereotypical images conveyed by history books, has had a major impact on the way we have been perceived by other Americans. We are still seen as dependent people and I wanted to say that there is another perspective. We, as Native Americans, must write our own history and stories. We must get the message out through all forms of media, through books, through documentation on the Internet, cable TV, films, workshops, and at meetings. Otherwise we'll continue to be victimized and stereotyped. With greater access to the mass media today we should be able to achieve greater understanding of who we are as a people.

I am an optimist. There is always hope for the improvement of human relations. This is how I perceive my mission in life. This is why I have supported the work and organization of intertribal conferences and I have broadened the scope of my activities to reach out to other tribes and also to other countries.

I tried teaching for a while, at the University of Utah, from 1976 to 1980. My older daughter, Emily, was already born then and I was the youngest faculty member. I could easily have obtained tenure. But I realized that teaching was not what I wanted to do. I wanted to get out of the academic Ivory Tower.

Then I went through a divorce and I was working on a research project in Washington, D.C. when I met my second husband, David Harrison, a lawyer. I realized that I wanted to defend Indian rights, making use of my historical knowledge and ability to conduct historical research. Professor Fred Nicholson, a historian from the University of Maryland, encouraged me and supported my idea. He thought I could work on Indian land and water rights.

I resigned from the University of Utah and opened my own company, Tiller Research, Inc. (TRI) in 1981. Research became my main business. I had to get research contracts, and to have creative and productive ideas.

JR: Tiller Research, your consulting company, has been involved in a wide variety of activities, mostly dealing with tribal rights. You have been doing research in support of Indian rights in many different fields, mostly in the West. You also had been working closely with your tribe, inter alia, during the celebration of its centennial in 1987.

VT: I remember very well that, in 1987, before my tribe's centennial, I went to my Tribal Council and proposed to organize a celebration to mark the hundredth anniversary of the establishment of our reservation. I became coordinator of that important event. I also remember the first research project that got my consulting company off the ground. We did historical research for a water rights case for the Rocky Boy Cree tribe of Montana. I teamed up with other historians and anthropologists. Since this case, we have worked on other water rights cases for tribes in Montana, California, Colorado, and New Mexico.

My research company is based in New Mexico. I live in an urban setting in Albuquerque. But I often go back to the reservation, in Dulce. Both my daughters, Emily Tiller Fredericks and Christina Harrison, have been through the traditional Apache Puberty Feasts. I move freely between the two environments, urban and tribal, and I also enjoy attending university symposiums and participating in international activities in Europe. Over the years, I have made a lot of friends in Europe, particularly in France.

In 2008, my company worked on an Indigenous film festival on the environment, in cooperation with the National Tribal Environment Council (NTEC). That festival obtained the support of UNESCO and the right to use its logo, rarely delivered, as recognition of the importance to protect our Indigenous territories. I went to UNESCO in Paris to report on the festival and explore the possibilities of distributing or showing some of those films in cultural institutions in Europe and at the United Nations in Geneva.

My company has worked on a wide variety of projects, including museums and architectural firms. While the National Museum of the American Indian was getting off the ground, we worked with a number of Native architects who contributed to the finalization of the research facility in Suitland, Maryland. More recently, we have worked on new legal issues, including the implementation of the National Historic Preservation Act, sharing information with the concerned tribes. In the 1980s we set up the BowArrow Publishing Company, as a division of TRI. That name was inspired by the famous Apache sculpture of Allan Houser, whom I met at the time. Through this new division we started conducting national research for the publication of *Tiller's Guide to Indian Country*.

JR: Do you feel that you have exceeded your childhood dreams? And are there some dreams that you still want to transform into realities?

VT: I certainly have accomplished more that I dreamt about when I was a child. I think I have done my part; that is, I have contributed to changing the perspective on Indian history and the image of contemporary Indians. I have brought up my two daughters and involved my family in many of my endeavors. I also have respected tribal traditions and honored the elders.

I still have a lot of projects. Having worked with the International Indigenous Environmental Festival I would like to promote the Native film industry in New Mexico, in order to create an active forum leading to the presentation and defense of the Native perspective on the environment, to support Native American filmmakers, and prevent global warming as much as possible. Our most recent festival occurred in October 2010.

I also would like to start a movement toward healing among Native Americans, especially those who suffered from the trauma of boarding school experiences. I actually have already started that movement on my reservation. We have talking circles, we discuss the historical trauma linking how we were brought up without learning anything about our own history, and not being allowed to speak our native language. We had good attendance at the local community level.

I also would like to create a body of tribal literature. We would like to be selective. Only studies worthy of publication would be considered. Right now we are interested in some stories by women leaders from the Pacific Northwest and we are planning to extend that project to the rest of the country.

I have been around strong women all my life. Apaches are a matriarchal society. History books project misconceptions about subservient Native women. We have been raised to be competent in everything we did. Our men also worked in the house. We had complementary roles.

This is how I have tried to bring up my two daughters, to be strong and independent. As for myself, I have finally realized that blaming white people is an obstacle to the full realization of my most fulfilling dreams. We have to let go of prejudice. This is the best way to be really free and create an understanding among all peoples of the world.

CHAPTER SEVEN

Erma Vizenor, tribal chair, White Earth Reservation, Minnesota

Erma Vizenor (Anishinaabe [Chippewa]) is a soft-spoken but very determined person. She is the first woman to lead the White Earth Anishinaabe Nation, the largest tribe in Minnesota.

Elected in 2004, Erma heralded in a new era of leadership that promoted fairness, transparency, and stability in tribal government. She has always taken risks to fight for justice and reform. In 1991 Erma took a stand against corruption and was jailed after a takeover of the tribal headquarters, which started the five-year reform movement known as Camp Justice that led to the conviction and imprisonment of the tribal chairman and two tribal council members for embezzlement, bid rigging, election fraud, and money laundering.

The White Earth Reservation, like other Anishinaabe reservations in Minnesota (Fond du Lac, Bois Forte, Grand Portage, Leech Lake, and Mille Lacs) is federally recognized. The Minnesota Chippewa tribe is a federation of the six Anishinaabe reservations. The Red Lake Reservation resisted the Dawes General Allotment Act, own their land in common, have their own constitution, and are not a part of the federation. White Earth, located in Northern Minnesota, near the source of the Mississippi River (Lake Itasca), was established by treaty in 1867. It has a new constitution, ratified by delegates in April 2009. The White Earth Nation is pursuing self-governance and independence from all governments that have been oppressive and paternalistic. As tribal chair for twenty-two thousand citizens, Erma is also striving for economic self-sufficiency. It's a difficult challenge: less than ten percent of the original treaty land is Indian-owned and the rate of unemployment is sixty to seventy percent.

Erma Vizenor has become one of the most famous White Earth citizens, with George Mitchell, activist and the first Anishinaabe candidate to run for alderman in

Erma Vizenor *(Photo by Nicolas Rostkowski)*

Minneapolis; Kimberly Blaeser, poet and professor of literature (University of Wisconsin); and the writer, Gerald Vizenor. Other famous Anishinaabeg include AIM leader Dennis Banks, and painters George Morrison (from Grand Portage) and David Bradley.[1]

Joëlle Rostkowski: You have become the tribal leader of the reservation of White Earth, where you were born. You are currently going through your second elected term. You appear as a key political Anishinaabe figure, brought to power after a difficult period of fraud and corruption. You started your professional life as a respected teacher in your own community and you were eventually appointed tribal secretary/treasurer. What led you to get involved in politics and what is your educational background?

Erma Vizenor: I have a Bachelor of Science degree in elementary education (cum laude), a Master of Science degree in guidance and counseling, and a CAGS in educational administration, superintendent of schools. A Bush Leadership Fellowship gave me the opportunity to earn a second master's degree in community decision-making and lifelong learning, and Doctor of Education degree in administration, planning, and social policy from Harvard University. Given all of my educational accomplishments, my most important work has been among my people of the White Earth tribe.

My life has been devoted to education. I was a teacher and school administrator on the White Earth Reservation for twenty years. The need in education was so great. I wanted to contribute every ounce of my soul to improve the education of

Indian children. High school dropout rates were ninety-five to one hundred percent in my home community where I started to teach.

As I worked for change in education, I realized that politics were integral to the systemic change that needed to happen in education. I saw the "haves" and the "have-nots" in tribal politics, the system of patronage and oppression. As a young educator, I became involved in the Democratic Party (DFL) politics, lobbying in St. Paul for education. Everything I was involved with, even my church leadership, I witnessed politics in action. Politics can't be separated from anything.

As a tribal leader, my priority is to improve the lives of Indian people. I have a special commitment to education, which I believe is the great equalizer in today's world.

I also work closely with the White Earth elders, who asked me in 1991 to be their spokesperson against the corruption and embezzlement within the tribal council.

I had just returned home from Harvard in June 1991, unpacking my books and computer, ready to write my dissertation, when the elders came to my door with a gift of tobacco and asked for my help. I could not refuse. After the elders left that evening, I wrote a press statement, spoke to the media the following morning, and organized a three-day sit-in at the White Earth tribal headquarters. On the third day of the sit-in, twenty-nine of us were arrested for criminal trespass and taken to jail. I was arrested and jailed two more times that summer.

Eventually, with the support of the late Senator Paul Wellstone, an investigation was conducted. Over a period of five years, I traveled all over the state of Minnesota, the United States, and the world asking for help. My doctoral dissertation had been put aside for activist work in justice for the people of White Earth. I met with the Bureau of Indian Affairs, congressional people in Washington, and the FBI. I linked up with peace and justice movements throughout the country.

In August 1996, a grand jury issued indictments against three tribal council members, including the tribal chairman. A week following the indictments, Harvard University wrote a letter to me that stated I had one academic year to finish my dissertation or I would be dropped from my doctoral program.

My work for justice had been accomplished at White Earth. An investigation had been completed, indictments were issued, and the corrupt tribal leaders were going to federal court. I packed my bags and computer and boarded a plane for Harvard to get my dissertation done before spring 1996. All within seven months, I had to review my literature again, write a new proposal for my dissertation, conduct my research, and write the dissertation. I accomplished all of it. By April 1, 1996, the draft of my dissertation passed my committee at Harvard. Immediately, I made travel plans for my family to attend my graduation ceremony at Harvard in June 1996.

On my return trip from graduation at Harvard, I had a stay-over in St. Paul where I was the final and last witness in the corruption trial of the three tribal officials. The three tribal leaders were convicted in federal court for a litany of felonies committed against the White Earth people.

Following the convictions of the tribal leaders, I was appointed secretary/treasurer of the White Earth tribe for an unexpired term. In January 1998, my husband and best friend passed away suddenly. I was grieved and lonely. I ran for reelection in the secretary/treasurer election in 1998 and served until 2002.

I lost my reelection for secretary/treasurer by a few votes in 2002 and was devastated because I felt I had let down so many people. Worst of all, I was politically blacklisted by the new tribal chairman and his regime in power and I could not get a job on the reservation. I was unemployed.

After my reelection loss in 2002, I went into seclusion at my home for a year, living off the small savings that I had accumulated. I prayed to God every day to guide me and help me. My two wonderful daughters tried to encourage and support me. I had always been their stronghold. Now they were holding me up.

My youngest daughter said to me, "Mother, you have the greatest education in the world. You are smarter and more capable than anyone. Get a normal job and don't ever go back to tribal politics. If you go back to tribal politics, I will personally come home and tie you up."

After a year of reflection I decided it was time to move on. I put my home up for sale and began to search for a job near Duluth where my youngest daughter and her family lived. I interviewed for a position at the Episcopal Church in New York. My home had several interested buyers but no sale.

In January 2004 my supporters came and asked me to run for tribal chairman. I filed and won the run-off in the primary election, beating the incumbent chairman. Being a spiritual person with faith as my foundation, I knew God had His hand on me for some reason I did not understand. I knew this time was pivotal for me and my tribe.

Ironically, my opponent in the 2004 general election was the former corrupt and convicted chairman who had gone to prison for seventeen felonies against the White Earth tribe. He had won the primary election to run against me.

Immediately after my primary election win, the media were at my home. They had my history of five years in Camp Justice and how my opponent was sent to prison. The media interviewed the former chairman. It was the biggest and most interesting campaign in Minnesota: The Reformer and the Felon Face Off.

The campaign started rough. Threats were made against my life. My husband wasn't there to support, protect, and help me. My daughters worried about me. I told my daughters, "I am not foolish. I will be careful but I will never show fear because once I show fear, I am licked, defeated, and done." In the campaign, I wanted to focus on issues. The media wanted to focus on the two "enemies" vying for the top leadership of the largest tribe in Minnesota. I had to borrow the money to hire a public relations firm to handle the media for me, which was a good decision.

My opponent, the former chairman, focused his campaign on the old patronage system that benefited his political favorites. I focused on issues and promised to be the "most honest, the highest principled, and the hardest working tribal chief that White Earth tribe has ever known."

Many supported me, including the former U.S. Attorney who prosecuted the corrupt chairman in federal court. The U.S. Attorney wrote an editorial in newspapers throughout the state that reminded readers how the former chairman bilked his tribe. I included the editorial in my campaign letters to tribal voters. All enrolled tribal members, living on and off White Earth Reservation, are eligible to vote.

In the general election of 2004, the former chairman, my opponent, beat me by a few votes on the White Earth Reservation. I believed that he still had a base of supporters who wanted patronage and corruption back. When the off-reservation votes were counted, I won by a landslide. I will never forget election night when I became the first woman chief of the tribe. My daughters and grandkids celebrated with me.

I wished for my husband to share this happy time. I gave ultimate thanks to God and vowed to keep my promise of honesty, fairness, and hard work.

Those who voted against me were in a state of fear and despair. Past chairmen who had won elections "cleaned house" and fired their enemies. Turmoil and instability had been the standard of the past. In my inaugural speech I reaffirmed my leadership for a new era in the history of White Earth. There would be fairness, stability, transparency, and healing. I fired no one.

Although people didn't believe me at the time, I have kept my word and walked my talk. I pledged a new day for all. I made amends and took the first step in forgiveness. I gave respect and grace whenever and wherever I went. And I worked hard for all.

My youngest daughter who had told me she would come home to tie me up if I went into tribal politics again was the proudest person in the tribe. She said, "Mom, you are always right and that's why Dad, Jody (my other daughter), and I always admire and love you. You are the strongest and wisest woman I know."

In 2008, I ran for reelection as tribal chair, an election that I won by sixty-seven percent of the popular vote in the primary election. I did not have to go through the general election.

I never take my political office for granted. I simply work hard and do all I can to make White Earth a better tribe.

My days, months, and years as a tribal leader are far from easy. Not everyone likes me. A few do not like a woman chief. I am a visionary, progressive leader, which infuriates those who do not want change.

I have lived and worked all of my life on the reservation. I know the politics here like I know my own two hands. I have seen the fear and intimidation of dictator leaders and their patronage. I have seen the insecurity of people, even the children in my classroom worried their parent would get fired. Before I was tribal chair, jobs were always given on favoritism and a patronage system, not by qualifications or competence, which is a reason the tribe has not progressed economically.

I was fortunate to have acquired a good education, therefore, I had freedom to speak out against injustice and to be resolute to fight for ethical principles.

When I advocate for education, I always say, "Education will give you a life of choices, not circumstances." It is so true. Without education or poorly educated, too many on the reservation are captives of circumstances, easily controlled, and subject to patronage.

JR: What have been the most important objectives of the tribal council under your leadership?

EV: We have been striving to establish stability, to create new jobs, to support our tribal college, to encourage and regulate our natural resources, to develop alternative sources of energy, to establish a transportation system that serves all the villages scattered throughout this large reservation. The WEEDO (White Earth Economic Development Office) works to support entrepreneurships on the reservation, to encourage partnerships and collaboration with surrounding counties and state. Fostering economic development on the reservation is a difficult task. We have been hurt by a faltering economy. We have so many economic and social problems that it seems like going through the Great Depression on a permanent basis. Critical needs on the reservation are jobs, housing, better schools and education, and good healthcare.

Some federal stimulus funds are available for Indian tribes that can be used for infrastructure and tax credits for new projects in Indian country. We do our best to apply for all funds and projects.

I put an emphasis on education. In 1997, I initiated the establishment of the White Earth Tribal and Community College. It is a liberal arts institution, tribally controlled, that emphasizes both traditional culture and cultural diversity. It offers two-year degrees. If offers specialized training and awareness programs, distance learning, Anishinaabe language classes, and adult education courses such as the General Equivalency Diploma (high school diploma). It has a nursing school. The tribal college received full accreditation in 2008.

We also have a new treatment and recovery facility for Indian youth in Bemidji, Minnesota. Many young people on the reservation and in Minnesota have problems with alcohol, drugs, and suffer from emotional or behavioral problems.

We hope federal policy will have a positive role in the support of tribal economies. In the past, the federal government has left us with false promises. During the assimilation and relocation period, the federal government gave one-way tickets to Indians to get them off the reservation. Most Indians ended up in the ghettos of large cities, worse off than on the reservation.

The strongest and most positive social characteristics that we share as Indians are the family structures. Those who adapt well to life off the reservation and in urban areas come back to the reservation for family, celebrations, and cultural identity. Our annual June powwow and celebration is the anniversary of the signing of the 1867 treaty that established the White Earth Reservation. More than five thousand people return to White Earth for the celebration and powwow.

JR: Historically the Chippewa of Minnesota had to cede extensive tracts of land. Civil War Era treaties limited them to a number of reservations where the land was allotted. An important proportion of lands on the White Earth Reservation were ceded—legally or illegally—to non-Indians. How can you establish a self-sufficient economy in such conditions?

EV: We are a Woodlands people. We live in a very beautiful region with many lakes, rivers, prairies, and forests. We have attempted to exercise our treaty rights over the years. We manage and protect the limited areas of our natural resources and lands. There have been conflicts and court challenges. Our goal is to maintain and develop our natural resources and land. Land acquisition is one of our highest priorities.

Most of the land on the White Earth Reservation (ninety percent) is still owned by white individuals, counties, state, and federal governments. The Dawes General Allotment Act of 1887 was devastating for the White Earth Reservation as land was allotted to individual Indians who lost their allotments through theft and swindle. We want to recover our original land that once was ours. In 1986, Congress passed the White Earth Land Settlement Act (WELSA) that provided compensation to original allotees and their heirs for land that was illegally seized. The act provided $6.6 million for economic development and cleared the clouded titles of hundreds of white property owners on the White Earth Reservation. Most Indians today believe WELSA was not a fair deal for us.

The WELSA economic development funds were used to build the Shooting Star Casino in 1991. However, over a period of five years, during corruption at White Earth, an unscrupulous management company of the casino swindled the tribe of $10 million, which included the $6.6 million of WELSA funds. The recovery of the $10 million is now going through the court system.

The Shooting Star Casino, Hotel, and Event Center, located in Mahnomen, is the largest source of revenue for the tribe and the largest employer in the area. Gaming revenue is used for infrastructure, services, support for tribal college, and youth programs.

In March 2009, the White Earth tribe won a court case against Mahnomen County for illegally collecting property taxes on the Shooting Star Casino. The land where the casino is located was purchased with WELSA funds. The act provides a stipulation that land purchased with WELSA funds are tax exempt, trust status, and restored to status of 1867. The Shooting Star Casino is now in trust status as it should have been in 1991, saving the tribe millions and millions of dollars.

JR: The establishment of your reservation goes back to the Peace Policy of President Ulysses Grant. At that time, the Peace Policy led to the establishment of various Christian denominations on treaty reservations. What is the current situation of the reservation with regard to the revival of traditional religion on Indian land?

EV: On the White Earth Reservation we had a lot of missionaries, mostly Episcopalian and Roman Catholic faiths. We have churches on our reservation but we continue to practice our traditional spirituality, Midewewin, the Grand Medicine Society, the sacred way of life of our people.

We are in a renaissance of traditional spirituality. Many people who were converted to Christianity practice traditional spirituality at the same time. We have our ceremonies, feasts, and dances year around. Tribal people are a spiritual people. Our spirituality has ensured our survival over a history of genocide, warfare, and diseases. A spiritual people will never be defeated. So true of White Earth Nation of Anishinaabeg.

CHAPTER EIGHT

Louisita Warren, elder of
Santa Clara Pueblo, New Mexico

Louisita Warren, born in 1910, was a fine lady whose precious and precise memory encompassed almost a century. This interview took place in Santa Fe in 1987, where she was living with her son Dave and his family.[1] During that memorable conversation, she enjoyed evoking her childhood, spent in the pueblo of Santa Clara. She put the emphasis on the spirit of independence and loyalty that characterized her as a young girl and kept inspiring her during her whole life.

Warren, who was seventy-seven years old when I met her, seemed to enjoy being an elder and sharing her personal history. She had an impressive ability to put her own personal experience in perspective. Looking back at her education, she reflected on the complex sociopolitical framework of Santa Clara Pueblo and on the underlying religious tensions that she could sense in the community.

Her experience illustrates what the anthropologist Edward Dozier called the "compartmentalization" of Pueblo socioceremonial systems into two separate parts: the Indigenous system and the Christian system, established by the Franciscan missionaries.

Considering her successful life as a mother and a grandmother, she marveled at the accomplishments of her whole family. She was particularly proud of her son Dave, one of the presidents of the Institute of American Indian Arts (IAIA). Today Dave Warren is still very active as a consultant at the IAIA, the School of Advanced Research, and the NMAI.

Louisita Warren's memory is still alive in the hearts and minds of all those who loved and admired her. Her grandson, Alvin Warren, after graduating from Dartmouth University, went through an initiation into traditional religion at Santa Clara, settled in the pueblo with his family, and became, at a very early age, lieuten-

Louisita Warren *(Courtesy of Dave Warren)*

ant governor and tribal councilmember. He has assisted his tribe with mapping and reacquiring title to over sixteen thousand acres of its ancestral lands. At present, he is secretary of Indian Affairs for the state of New Mexico.

Joëlle Rostkowski: You have been brought up in Santa Clara Pueblo in the 1920s and now live with your family in Santa Fe. Life in the pueblos has changed drastically during the course of your life. Looking back, how would you define your identity?

Louisita Warren: I was brought up in Santa Clara in a very traditional way, at the beginning of the twentieth century, when Pueblo Indians still remained rather isolated geographically and culturally. During the first half of the century, the Catholic missions were very powerful.

I learned about my family history and my roots through our elders. We are Tewa people, like the people of San Ildefonso, Tesuque, Pojoaque, and Nambe. Although we don't speak exactly the same language, we understand each other and we still have intervillage ceremonies. All those pueblos had similar traditional social organizations. The members of each village were divided between the Winter and Summer People. They alternated seasonally in our tribal government. The Winter People took over the leadership after the harvest and remained in charge until spring. The dual division in moieties was also very important from a religious point of view. Children usually joined the moiety of their father, but membership always depended upon initiation.

Our family belonged to the Winter People. One of my uncles, who was very close to me, helped me understand our traditional rituals and transmitted to me many of our ancestral values. I received a dual education, traditional and Catholic, as was often the case in the pueblos. I went to church with my parents, who were Catholic and very respectful of the priests, but I knew that my uncle, whom I fondly called "the dear old man," was very critical of the role of the church.

JR: Did you find it difficult to cope with two strict education systems, the traditional system and the Catholic Church? How did you manage to conform to what was then expected from a young girl at that time?

LW: I remember that I wanted to be a good girl in both systems. But I had a strong personality and I was also very independent. At church, I was often noticed because I was very tall for my age. I liked church music and I enjoyed being a good singer. I also wanted to prove that I had learned the prayers and that I knew them by heart. But my mother taught me to remain discreet and quiet.

I found it difficult to accept the authoritarian behavior of the Catholic priest. He spoke Spanish, was often frowning in a deprecating way, and kept pointing his finger at us as if we had done something wrong. My father tried to comfort me and to explain that it had nothing to do with me: the priest was just telling us about heaven and hell, his mission was to teach us the difference between virtue and vice. With my father's help I tried to understand why the priest seemed to believe we could go to hell.

Many children wondered why the priest seemed so furious, as if he thought we were bad people and had done something terrible. In our culture we have no equivalent of the original sin. The Spanish priest did not speak our language and we could not establish any friendly communication with him.

Our history was marked by the Spanish conquest. In the sixteenth and the seventeenth centuries they came, bible in pocket, gun in hand, established a church in every pueblo and forbid any expression of traditional religion. The Pueblo Revolt drove the conquistadors out of New Mexico but they came back and reestablished Spanish rule.

My uncle, who was a traditional religious leader, told me that pueblo meetings in the kivas were outlawed and many kivas were destroyed. My ancestors were forced to accept the Church's authority and to bow and kneel before the image of the cross.

Christianity was imposed upon us. We had no other choice. Pueblo religion went underground and we became secretive, suspicious of outsiders. But there were also some convergences, some mutual influences, and some conversions. I know that, in our pueblo, some of us became very devout Christians, without necessarily giving up their traditional religion. But, for many others, conversion has been merely a screen, an acceptance hiding real beliefs. Conversion became a way to avoid direct confrontation, to cope with the presence of strangers on our land. My uncle used to tell me that Christianity was like a coat that we could wear to hide our traditional clothes.

I wanted to be a good girl in both systems and to please my parents, who often brought some food to the priest. In that respect, I often recall an anecdote, a story that I have kept in mind, as clearly as if it had happened yesterday! I had planted some pumpkin seeds, looking forward to eating a delicious pumpkin for Thanksgiving. The whole village was doing the same thing, in preparation for that important day. Many of them were brought to the church, where the priest was supposed to make a choice between the most beautiful ones.

My pumpkin was one of the biggest in the village. My mother congratulated me but asked me to give it to the priest. My father was reluctant to ask me to do that, but my mom insisted on that symbolic gesture of generosity. It was her way to give me a good education, a sense of sharing, but it was my turn to be really furious. I still remember a strong feeling of frustration and fear. Fear because I was clearly conscious of my selfishness and of my anger. Of course I thought of hell. I remembered the priest's finger pointing at me and I was terribly scared. The priest understood all that, just by looking at me, but he said nothing.

JR: After being brought up in Santa Clara you got married and settled in Santa Fe. Has spiritual life remained very important for you in an urban setting and have you remained very close to your traditional values?

LW: After the death of my parents I left Santa Clara Pueblo and I also stopped going to church. That was an unusual decision in our family. Many of my relatives are fervent and practicing Christians. I respect their beliefs. Looking back I feel that my position has a lot to do with my uncle's influence. But I know that it can be explained by the fact that I had been looking for an ideal church. A church having the power to fulfill my dreams.

In our family, some devout Christians have chosen the Protestant church. But are they really and totally accepted by their religious community? One of my cousins was not allowed to be buried in the church cemetery. As far as I am concerned, I know I don't want to be buried in the Catholic Church's cemetery. It's not because, in many ways, I am a rebel, but just because I have other plans. We have a very beautiful piece of land at Santa Clara. I would like to be cremated and my ashes put in a beautiful pot made in our village. The pot would be put on a small hill, where one could think that many other pots and a lot of ashes could be found.

The pot, wrapped up in a nice embroidered piece of cloth, will be placed where all the members of my family will be able to find me. I won't need flowers but I will be happy if somebody could plant some seeds, so that a small garden could grow around the pot. This is the image I would like to leave. This is how I would like all of them to think of me, in peace on that hill, hoping they will remember my best qualities and will forgive my weaknesses. Animals will come to see me, they will eat the flowers and I'll listen to the rain falling and the wind blowing. I know I will.

This is my dream. I believe in life after death, I believe there is another world in which our problems just vanish. I believe in a Supreme Being, whatever the representation of that divine power might be.

JR: Looking back to your past, beyond your education at Santa Clara and your active and happy family life in Santa Fe, are there important events that have shaped or influenced your vision of the world and your spiritual life?

LW: I have been through several crises in my life and I feel that I have learned a lot from those critical moments.

For example, in my late forties—I think I was forty-seven then—I realized that something in my education was missing. I decided then to go to university. My husband was an educator and he had always told me that reading would enrich my life considerably. He also thought that books would keep me company after his death. I realized that he was absolutely right. I have taken advantage of my university training to reinforce the dialogue within my own family. My son Dave had become an important man who had a lot of responsibilities and I wanted to be able to communicate with him, and also with his wife and with my grandchildren.

Much more recently I went through a different kind of crisis. I fell and broke my leg. I had complications from the surgery and, for some reason, the wound would not heal. Amputation was then considered. I refused and they warned me that I could die. I thought it was the end and I began to prepare myself for it. Friends and neighbors came to visit me and started praying for me. I even remember a Protestant minister who came to see me and comfort me.

One day I looked at my leg and I saw that skin regeneration was under way. I was suddenly filled with hope.

I knew that it was the beginning of a gradual recovery period and that I was going to heal. Whenever I face a difficult period, a moment of trial, I try to concentrate on an inner vision. My imagination usually takes me to a beautiful landscape, often to Peru, to its snowy summits. Strangely enough, my mind wanders to that faraway land, although I have never been to Peru. But I have seen images of those mountains and listened to the sound of the native flute and I find comfort in them. They give me a lot of courage when I feel bad. That is how I recover my peace of mind.

JR: You have a cozy Santa Fe home, very close to your son's family house, where he lives with his wife and two children. You seem to have established a good balance between your family life, an active social life, and a very intense inner existence.

LW: I know that I love and need my family, and that I enjoy having a social life. I would not like to be isolated and live far from those I love. My family and my friends give me a lot of support. Many people come to see me and I always insist on approaching them with open-mindedness and tolerance. They give me a lot and I do think I also have something to give them. There is respect and reciprocity in our relationships. I strongly believe that there is nothing worse than putting somebody else down.

One day I will have the inner feeling that my life is coming to an end and I'll be getting ready to leave this world.

I have grandchildren and I have kept the values of my village, Santa Clara Pueblo, even though I live in Santa Fe. My life is like a tapestry: some of its patterns are striking and colorful while others are less intense, less interesting. I have reached a point in my life when I feel that I am not far from the border. As my dear uncle used to tell me: "Death is a handsome young man. In His time, he will come . . ."

Today when I look back at my life, and when I reflect on my values and my beliefs, I know that the whole universe is my church, that the birds are its choir and that my faith is unfailing. I also know that, if I was given the opportunity to live a second life and to select my identity, I would choose to be Indian once again. It has been a beautiful experience!

CHAPTER NINE

Tony Abeyta, painter and sculptor

Tony Abeyta (Navajo) is a gifted artist whose serenity and self-confidence are remarkable. There is something of the Navajo quest for harmony, wholeness (hozho), in his approach to life. Modesty and ambition are reconciled in the way he likes to present himself. And he asserts his Navajo identity as strongly as his desire to belong to the global art scene.

His life is a success story. He is discreet concerning the obstacles he may have encountered occasionally as an artist. He likes to say that, whenever the future looked uncertain, something came up that allowed him to find new collectors, new opportunities to exhibit his works, new possibilities to travel, explore the world, and enrich his artistic experience.

This interview took place in Paris on June 6, 2009, the sixty-fifth anniversary of D-Day. As we were talking, President Obama and his family were being driven to Notre Dame Cathedral. Tony Abeyta remembered that his father, during the war, was among a group of code talkers. He had suffered shell shock and had a difficult time recovering from it.[1]

Joëlle Rostkowski: How do you like to define yourself?

Tony Abeyta: I define myself as a contemporary Native American artist. I don't define myself as a traditional person. I was born and raised in an urban setting, in Gallup. My father, Narciso Abeyta, came from the Navajo reservation, where he lived until the age of sixteen. He was a well-known and respected painter, often presented as a disciple of Dorothy Dunn—the famous Native American Indian art teacher—and part of the easel movement that developed in Santa Fe before the Second World War. After returning from the war in the South Pacific, and trying to recover from shell shock, he stopped painting for ten years.

Tony Abeyta *(Photo by Nicolas Rostkowski)*

As for my mother, she was Anglo, coming from a Quaker family. She was also an artist, working with ceramics, and she was a good weaver, having learned Navajo traditional skills.

JR: Looking back at your childhood, thinking of your dreams and comparing them with the present reality, do you think that having parents who were artists led you to become a painter and do you feel that you have accomplished your childhood dreams?

TA: I was brought up in a very creative and artistic atmosphere but, as a teenager, I remember that I rather dreamt of becoming a filmmaker or an architect. I had the opportunity to study at the IAIA, Institute of American Indian Arts, founded in Santa Fe in the 1960s. It was a wonderful institution, intertribal, offering training in various artistic fields and it was totally free.

I got a grant from the Navajo tribe and I remember that the IAIA provided everything we needed: paint, brush, lodging, etc. At the IAIA I met Indians from all over the country and some of the painters that have become famous since then. Allan Houser, the famous Apache sculptor, was teaching there. Darren Vigil Gray, another Apache artist, had just graduated. There was a free spirit of creativity and cooperation. I am part of a very creative Native American artistic movement, encouraged by IAIA that has trained and promoted David Bradley, Emmi Whitehorse, Jaune Quick to See Smith.

I considered going to the Rhode Island School of Design but I finally decided to go to the Maryland Institute College of Arts in Baltimore. Meanwhile, I was already selling paintings. I remember the first painting I sold, at the age of eighteen.

I also clearly remember that it was in 1985—I was not twenty years old yet—when I attended an exhibition at the Fine Arts Museum in Santa Fe that I found my way. I then saw all the promising and already confirmed Native artists gathered in a splendid show: Allan Houser, R. C. Gorman, David Bradley, T. C. Cannon. I wanted to be like them. It was a critical moment for me. That's when I decided that I wanted to be a painter.

It was thrilling to be able to meet all those striking personalities. It was an ebullient atmosphere and there was more cooperation than competition. R. C. Gorman, as the most famous Navajo artist, was very generous with the younger generation.

Allan Houser was an excellent teacher and partner. But I think my favorite was the late T. C. Cannon: brilliant artist and poet. He was fascinating, paving new ground, uniting Native traditions and pop art with a great deal of humor.

JR: Although Santa Fe is at the core of your education, your studies took you to many different places and to several big cities: Baltimore, New York, Chicago, and to Europe: Florence and Venice, the South of France.

TA: Yes. I think that—perhaps unconsciously—I have sought inspiration through travel. I was studying perspective in Baltimore when I saw a poster offering an opportunity to go to France. It was in Lacoste, between Avignon and Aix en Provence. In Lacoste I did sculpture, working with limestone, travertine, and marble. Then when my roommate left for Florence, I went with him and I studied and worked there, with the help of a generous man, Jules Maidoff, who paid part of the tuition fees that I couldn't afford, just because he wanted to help a Native American artist. He was also an artist himself.

In Italy, I studied art history, the Renaissance, and I spent my time visiting museums. I was drawn to the Flemish portraits, the Renaissance masters—Piero della Francesca, Veronese, Botticelli, Michelangelo—but I also revisited masterpieces from Egypt and Greece. I still vividly recall the emotion and admiration I felt while looking at the perfect beauty of some Greek sculptures.

I was always drawn to the elsewhere. I studied and worked in New York and then I moved with my wife to Chicago. We already had a son, my first wife was a fashion designer, and we always managed to live well without worrying about financial problems. I have always had opportunities to sell my works and live as an artist without having to teach or do another job. I was never afraid of being poor.

I am always learning and I am always in movement. My attachment to where I come from, the Southwest, and the lively art scene from that region never deterred me from exploring the world and learning more about art. I want to experiment with various mediums and images from many different sources of inspiration. What keeps me going, at the age of forty-three, is that I remain and will always remain a student of art.

JR: The Southwest, its strong colors, its animals and plants, the traditional deities of the Navajos, sometimes reinterpreted in an abstract manner, are an integral part of your work. But, over the last few years you have started to work with charcoal and ink, creating those "flower bombs" in black and white, that have been so successful.

TA: Although I was always drawn to colors, working with natural pigments, sand and oil paint, to capture the essence of Southwestern landscapes and Native traditions, I enjoy working with a new palette in my black and white works that have been very well received. I cling to the diversity of expression: abstract paintings, landscape painting, murals, sculptural paintings in three dimensions. I consider myself as a sort of alchemist working in mixed media and experimenting with new forms. I feel I can forge new paths in Native American art.

For me, art is an energy. That energy goes through me as it flows through other artists. It's a force that we have to transmit and express. It's not ours. We are instruments of that force.

I create from a Native American vocabulary but I am inspired by the knowledge I have acquired from other parts of the world, and from various periods of art history, whether it be Flemish portraits, the Italian Renaissance, and, among contemporary artists, the sculptor Rodin and of course, Picasso. Picasso has been a liberating influence. Among contemporary American artists, I feel that Rothko, with the pulsing intensity of his paintings, has deeply influenced me.

I never want to be called predictable. My cultural experiences keep growing, extending to the East. I think my paintings function like mandalas. I experiment with images—personal, tribal, and universal. I like to stand at cultural crossroads. I think that what has kept me going was being and remaining a student of art. Sometimes I feel I am six different artists all working together.

I consider myself as an urban Indian and a traditionally inspired Navajo. I paint the colors and textures of my homeland but my exposure to other artists somehow is integrated into my work.

JR: You have had a personal retrospective at the Southwest Museum in Los Angeles in 2000. You have had a recent exhibition in Paris in June 2009 (Galerie Orenda). Your work has been integrated into important private and public collections. What goals do you think you want to achieve now?

TA: I do not want to rest on my laurels. I feel I have a responsibility as a Native artist. One of the basic foundations of my work is Nature. My work is nature based. Its focal source is the colors of the earth. I want it to remain organic, botanical. But I keep expanding my experiences. I even acquired experience as a gallery owner for a while. I had a gallery in Taos because I wanted to be exposed to the business side of the art world. There is always something new to learn. Right now I think I might consider living in Paris for a while. Facing success is not a problem. Paintings are dreams that you can share and I'll keep nourishing my dreams.

Tony Abeyta is one of the leading young Native painters. He has won many prizes at the Southwestern Association of Indian Arts (SWAIA) and been exhibited nationwide and abroad. His work is part of prestigious private collections and museum collections, including the National Museum of the American Indian in Washington, D.C.; the Institute of American

Indian Arts in Santa Fe, New Mexico; and the Heard Museum in Phoenix, Arizona.

In his retrospective at the Heard Museum in 2008, he declared that he wanted to "abstractly render the Navajo underworld, draw the realm we live in today and draw our relationship to the cosmos."

Selected exhibitions

2010: *Wonderland*, Gallery Orenda, Paris, France, collective show. Blue Rain Gallery, Annual Indian Market Exhibition

2009: *Sonate des deux Mondes*, Gallery Orenda, Paris, France, Carré des Arts; Blue Rain Gallery, Annual Indian Market Exhibition

2008: *Underworldness*, Heard Museum of Art, one-person exhibition; *Black and White Drawings*, Sculpture Objects and Functional Art (SOFA, New York); Blue Rain Gallery, Santa Fe Annual Indian Market Exhibition; Navy Pier Art Show, Chicago.

2004: National Museum of the American Indian, opening, Washington, D.C., multi-panel, *Anthem*, chosen as the official image, displayed on banners and on official posters.

2000: Southwest Museum, Los Angeles County Museum of Art, ten-year retrospective, featuring forty pieces from public and private collections.

CHAPTER TEN

David Bradley, painter and sculptor

David Bradley is an Anishinaabe (Chippewa) artist, born in Minnesota, who has spent most of his life in New Mexico. He is a sensitive and rather somber man, a master of political satire, whose work is filled with madcap historical and pop culture references.

Bradley defines his sense of humor as specifically Indian, closely linked to his Anishinaabe background and the traditional trickster stories still very much alive in his community. Throughout his career as an artist—both painter and sculptor—he has revisited American history, Native history, and major cultural references and icons of contemporary life.

He is one of the most remarkable artists of his generation. This interview took place in Santa Fe in 2009, thirty years after he graduated, first in his class, at the Institute of American Indian Arts (IAIA). He reflects on his career, his paintings, and on his fifth one-man museum exhibit, organized at the Nicolaysen Art Museum, in Wyoming (January 23–May 10).

David Bradley's work, exhibited in several museums, is also reproduced and praised in many art history books. His work is significant, meticulous, mostly representational, often baroque and—although humorous—it conveys a very sharp political message.[1]

Joëlle Rostkowski: You are a sculptor and a painter, a Native artist whose works address American history and many contemporary issues. Do you like to define your-self as a Native artist or do you prefer to be integrated into the mainstream of contemporary art?

David Bradley: It depends on the context. I remember that, when I was an art student, I was rather drawn to sculpture. Actually that's how I started, as a sculp-tor, working with various materials: stone and clay, often cast in bronze and wood.

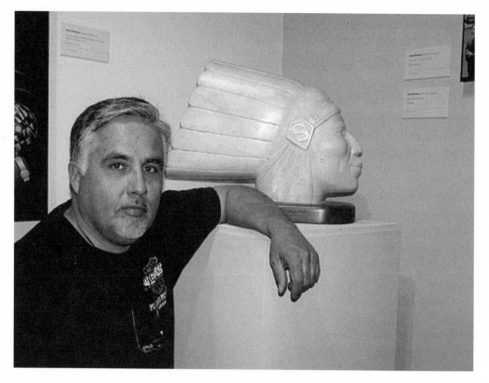

David Bradley *(Photo by Dennis Culver)*

Although I never gave up sculpture, I became known almost exclusively as a painter. But I do like to define myself as both sculptor and painter and as a Native artist whose work deals with many historical and contemporary issues of mainstream society.

JR: Your work has a very strong historical and political content. It can be looked at as a Native reappropriation of history, through an ironic representation of many historical characters such as General Custer, but also as a reappropriation of universal cultural icons such as the Mona Lisa, reinterpreted as an Indian princess.

DB: My paintings are also sociopolitical statements. Because of their history and their current problems, Indian people are political by definition. I perceive myself both as an artist and as an Indian rights activist inviting collectors and art lovers to reconsider history and contemporary society.

Actually, over the years, as Native American artists were asserting themselves and as the market for Indian art was developing, there were controversies as to the appropriate way to define who is Indian. There is the legal definition, the tribal definition, and the public definition. The public definition is usually wrong because it is so often based upon stereotypes. But it must be added that even Indian people themselves sometimes have erroneous assumptions about themselves.

A long time ago we were clearly identified as belonging to a certain ethnic group. Now Indian identity has become a political concept. It has little to do with race and ethnicity but rather with the sovereignty of Indian nations. We are citizens of a particular Indian community.

JR: You have firmly expressed your views when the status of American Indian artists was at the center of a sociopolitical and legal debate, in the 1970s and 1980s. That debate finally led to the adoption of the Indian Arts and Crafts Act of November 29, 1990. It was a law adopted to protect the Native American art market from fraud. According to that law, "to be considered an Indian artist, the individual artist or craftsperson must be a member of an Indian tribe, or must be certified as an Indian artisan by an Indian tribe."

DB: The appeal of Native arts and the development of a booming and profitable market had led over the years to abusive appropriation of Native identity by outsiders. I put my own reputation on line when I took a firm position in favor of strengthening laws that protect our Native communities from fraud and fake Indian artists. In so doing I was not afraid to step on some people's toes. I am convinced it was a good cause and it was necessary to defend it.

   The current definition is appropriate. Today Native nations define membership, but Indian artists who are not enrolled can also obtain a certificate attesting that they are an artist/artisan of a specific tribe. Everybody knows who they are in that particular community.

   For expressing my views about fake Indian artists, I have been blacklisted in some circles. I often joke about the Black Queen of Native Arts. It's not only a joke. An Indian mafia runs publicly funded exhibitions all around the country, rather secretly; they know how to work within the system and how to have access to government money. I don't regret taking a firm position in that respect.

JR: Your work is known for its irony, its sarcastic references to popular history, in particular the history of the West: the Noble Savage, the American spirit represented as a pack of cigarettes, cowboys and Indians, saloons, museum and gallery openings filled with coyotes, the Santa Fe Railway ending nowhere, nuns and missionaries dancing wildly together. It is as if you stood outside and put in evidence the violence and absurdity of historical conflicts and the tragi-comedy of human relations.

DB: Indian humor is sometimes close to black humor. Several tribes have a culture hero called the trickster. Among the Anishinaabe, our cultural trickster is Naanabozho. In my early career I have molded a ceramic representation of Naanabozho, a figure with a small head, very thickly bound braids, big hands, and huge moccasins. That was my interpretation of our tribal trickster.

   My paintings have been described as narrative art because, when I paint, I tell a story. Like trickster stories, my works are imbued with fantasies and incongruities. Maybe I am a trickster. People usually are struck by the fact that, although I am not a funny person, my paintings are very funny. Or, on the contrary they tell me that I am too serious and that my paintings should be more serious.

   Actually I think that I have a certain ironic vision of reality that is spontaneously reflected in my work. I like to say that life is ironic, it has beauty, chaos, intertwined elements of comedy and tragedy. And my work is about life, past and present.

JR: Gerald Vizenor, in an essay written for your exhibition at the Nicolaysen Art Museum in Wyoming, has made reference to your work as an expression of the Native baroque and coined the expression "Bradlarian baroque."[2]

DB: Yes. I like this definition. As a writer, Gerald Vizenor has this ability to create new expressions, to detect trends, to forge new concepts, to compare visions. He may have been struck by some of my chubby women and stocky men, who have definitely something in common with the Colombian painter Botero. But, beyond that, I think that he is making reference to my perception of the world and to the figures that come to life in my paintings. They are, as he says, contorted, whimsical, and eccentric. Gerald Vizenor has recognized a certain convergence of visions between his writings and my paintings. And he has selected some of my works to illustrate his book covers.

In that context, in the catalogue of the exhibit, I have noticed that he has specifically commented upon some specific works such as *The End of the Santa Fe Trail*, *How the West Was Lost*, *The Immaculate Assumption*, and *The Last Supper*, in which I enjoy playing on words and reappropriating famous artistic or historical themes.

Like me Gerald Vizenor is Anishinaabe and he sees in my paintings what he calls the satire of trickster stories on canvas.

JR: The title of the exhibition organized at the Nicolaysen Art Museum was *Restless Native, the Journey*. Mary Abbe wrote in the *Minneapolis Star Tribune* that you think of yourself as a "tumbleweed, rootless and impatient."[3] However you could also be described as a very quiet and philosophical man.

DB: I think that my restlessness and my impatience go into my paintings, although they are very elaborate and meticulous. Art is about expressing your feelings freely, following your heart. And making strong statements through the power of images.

Art is also a way to fight. Art is war. I see my life as an artist as a modern counterpart to a warrior's existence. In one of my artist's statements I said that through art I want to express the wonders and horrors and overall richness of reality. Victory comes when I manage to convey that reality.

JR: You have been brought up in an urban reservation, downtown Minneapolis. During your childhood and later on, at the university, did you live mostly among Indians or rather in mainstream society?

DB: My community was called Blue Earth and my school was on the edge of the Leech Lake Reservation. There was a mixture of kids in that school, mostly non-Indians. So I lived in both worlds. I was very quickly identified as someone who could draw and I participated in arts projects from the third or fourth grade. After graduating from high school I went to college in St. Paul, one of the Twin Cities, and then to the University of Tucson, Arizona. Those were universities with a majority of non-Indians but where the number of Indian students was increasing. There were also some striking personalities among the faculty, for example, best-selling author Vine Deloria Jr., who was then teaching in Tucson.

JR: You spent some time in the Peace Corps. That led you to live in some foreign countries. Were you influenced by the time spent abroad?

DB: I spent some time in Guatemala, in Haiti, and in Costa Rica. I learned Spanish and I broadened my experience as a human being and as a painter. I was very impressed by the Haitian painting renaissance, the bright colors, the vitality of their artistic movement. In Guatemala, where the majority of the population is Indian, I also was very interested in the arts and crafts. All that developed my interest in folk art. That interest was later extended to universal art history and to painters who have something in common with the folk art tradition: Douanier Rousseau, Eastern European folk painters, Japanese watercolor painters.

At the Institute of American Indian Arts in Santa Fe (IAIA) I was happy to be exposed to other Native traditions, to meet students from other reservations. I sometimes felt that we learned more from other students than from our teachers. We strengthened our identities. The very famous painter Fritz Scholder and the sculptor Allan Houser had already left the IAIA, but they kept in touch and visited the institute. Kevin Red Star, T. C. Cannon, Bob Haozous had already graduated but some of their work was regularly displayed. We could meet with them occasionally.

I participated in the group shows that IAIA organized and also in collective art exhibitions at the Heard Museum. All the IAIA students and graduates competed for prizes in various venues. I obtained the first prize for sculpture from the Red Cloud Heritage Center (Pine Ridge, South Dakota). I remember that it was a sculpture in pipestone, a reclining woman.

JR: How did you start your career as an artist exhibited in private galleries?

DB: I was very lucky because the Elaine Horwich Gallery, one of the major galleries in Santa Fe, expressed an interest in my work. It gave me, very early on, the opportunity to participate in a couple of shows with the already famous Fritz Scholder. Then I became one of the artists of that gallery. I was the youngest Native artist to have a one-man show in 1981 and I stayed with Elaine Horwich for some fifteen years, until 1994.

I kept in touch with museums and my work kept being exhibited by the IAIA. In Santa Fe, now that the Horwich Gallery has closed its doors, I work mostly with the Blue Rain Gallery. Some of my paintings have also been exhibited in Paris (*Go West*, Galerie Orenda, June 2008).

JR: Looking back at your achievements as an artist do you think that you have exceeded your childhood dreams?

DB: I have just celebrated thirty years of my career as an artist. Looking back, I think I didn't have very structured goals when I went to university and even when I started at the IAIA. Right now I keep raising the bar. And I want to keep learning.

I am attending a welding class at the community college. I keep extending my vision. I want to devote more time and energy to sculpture, mostly abstract. I would like to work on large pieces, in steel or other materials, which could be exhibited outside.

JR: Among your current projects do you envisage going abroad and broadening your perspective?

DB: I would enjoy going abroad, maybe to France for another exhibition, or to Italy where I have already enjoyed traveling with my wife and my son. There is an interesting community of artists in Tuscany, near Carrara, and I would like to be integrated into one of those groups as an artist in residence to further my experience as a painter.

"A STORIER WITH PAINT"

David Bradley has reinvented and reinterpreted the history of the West. He is both a popular and provocative artist, a "storier with paint," according to Gerald Vizenor. He "has a great talent for seeing more than most people see, politically and visually," Suzan Harjo has pointed out.

Bradley's work is in private and museum collections, including the Plains Art Museum (Fargo, North Dakota), the Tweed Museum of Art (University of Minnesota, Duluth), the Millicent Rogers Museum (Taos, New Mexico), and the University of Wyoming Art Museum (Laramie).

In 2008 a retrospective exhibition of his work was organized by the Nicolayen Art Museum (Casper, Wyoming) under the title: *Restless Native: The Journey*. Over the last ten years he has been widely exhibited nationally and internationally.

Selected exhibitions

2010: Blue Rain Gallery, Santa Fe, New Mexico. Featured Poster Artist, University of Warsaw, Poland.

2009: Blue Rain Gallery, solo exhibition.

2008: Blue Rain Gallery, solo exhibition; *Go West*, Gallery Orenda, Paris, France; Featured Poster Artist, 50th Anniversary, Heard Museum Indian Fair and Market, Phoenix, Arizona; *Changing Hands II*, Weisman Museum of Art, Minneapolis.

2007: *Native American Art*, District of Columbia Art Center, Washington, D.C.; *Changing Hands II*, Eiteljord Museum, Indianapolis, Indiana; *American Icons Through Indigenous Eyes*, District of Columbia Art Center, Washington, D.C.

2006: *West of Everywhere*, Nicolayen Museum, Casper, Wyoming. *Roy Lichtenstein / Native Pop*, Museum of Fine Arts, Santa Fe, New Mexico.

2005: *Iconolash*, Museum of Indian Arts and Culture, Santa Fe; *Changing Hands II*, Museum of Art and Design, New York.

2004: *Restless Native: Coming Home*, American Indian Neighborhood Development Corporation, Minneapolis, Minnesota; *Please Don't Touch the Indians*, Gene Autry Museum, Los Angeles, California.

2002: *Beyond Beads and Feathers*, Portland Art Museum, Oregon; *Postcard from Santa Fe: The Artwork of David Bradley*, University of Wyoming Art Museum.

2001: *Traditions and Visions*, Muckenthaler Museum, Fullerton, California; *A Vision of America*, Berlin Embassy, Germany.

CHAPTER ELEVEN

Darren Vigil Gray, painter and musician

Darren Vigil Gray (Jicarilla Apache) is a free spirit. He is an intense and inspired artist who refuses to accept conventions and compromise. He is both faithful to his Apache roots and determined to achieve his goals as an international artist and reach out to an international audience.

He has been befriended by famous pop stars such as the Beatles. Yet he doesn't hesitate to spend hours with his close circle of friends, to play music, to spend time with his family. When he comes to Paris, he always insists on visiting an elderly Apache gentleman and his French wife who keep waiting for his return.

As we are talking in his studio, in the outskirts of Santa Fe, we are listening to a vinyl recording of his mother's voice, whose immaculate and moving interpretation of classic opera melodies conjure up memories of Darren's past and accounts for his twofold passion, painting and music.[1]

Joëlle Rostkowski: You are a painter and a musician, born in New Mexico and still living there. You are also an Apache Indian brought up on the Jicarilla Reservation. You have become an urban Indian living in Santa Fe, married to Jill Momaday, N. Scott Momaday's daughter. You are a well-known artist and an international traveler and have many friends abroad. Your work has recently been exhibited in Paris. How do you like to define yourself?

Darren Vigil Gray: I always wanted as much freedom as possible and my feeling of freedom has been expressed both in painting and in music. I remember that when I was a child, on the Jicarilla Reservation in New Mexico, I was a sort of cowboy. My father was a rancher and that free, outdoor life was part of my education. Both my

Darren Vigil Gray *(Photo by Nicolas Rostkowski)*

parents were musical. My father, who was a rodeo cowboy and rancher, also had a country western band. He was very charismatic. He was our tribal leader and a lot of important people came to visit us. My mother loved music and was a good soprano. So I am a reservation boy, but I also had the opportunity to be initiated rather early to music, to visual arts, and to politics.

My exposure to music came early. I started classical piano. My exposure to the outside world was also part of my education. Through my father's involvement in politics and in musical activities I met people like Kirk Douglas and Johnny Cash. My father was occasionally involved in producing movies. Music led me to art. Actually the idea to become an artist came at a later stage, when I was a teenager. I remember that I somehow felt trapped on the reservation, although I had a lot of freedom.

This is why I left home at the age of fifteen. My parents had been through a difficult divorce. My brother was deeply hurt by that traumatic experience and, for him, recovery was a long process. I did not want to take sides in those family matters and I felt I had to find my own way. I had the opportunity to enroll at the Institute of American Indian Arts (IAIA) in Santa Fe and I seized it immediately. IAIA was then a boarding school, but I could cope with that. It was a very inspiring time for me. I didn't feel homesick. I was very excited and I started being in touch with a lot of extraordinarily accomplished artists from another generation—Fritz Scholder,

R. C. Gorman—while at the same time learning a lot about the history of art and contemporary European painting: Matisse, Picasso, de Kooning.

During my studies at the IAIA, I experimented with a lot of materials and a lot of styles. I gravitated around abstract expressionism, postmodernism. I tried many different styles while quickly developing contacts with galleries in Santa Fe in order to be directly in touch with collectors, tourists, and cultural institutions. Right now I still refuse to define my style. It's an ongoing process. I continue to explore. The natural world is the key element that gives me some balance.

I have to get inward, to investigate, to search for the best medium, the most satisfactory forms of expression. I have to make a lot of chaos in order to push things into shape.

JR: Nietzsche said, "You must have chaos within you to give birth to a dancing star." Is that how you perceive your creativity, the specific strength of your very powerful and intense landscapes and mysterious figures of crown dancers?

DVG: Exactly. I need the intensity, the movement, the delicate balance between my roots, the memory of Apache rituals, the fascinating beauty and mystery of the Southwest landscapes and some more private sources of inspiration like the beauty of my wife Jill, for example, and the harmony and strength of our family life in Santa Fe with our two daughters. My creativity is also constantly reinforced by my travels and my exposure to other artists and my experiments with new styles and new materials.

Movement has always been part of my life. Having left home early doesn't mean I have forgotten where I come from. I am still in touch with the Jicarillas, interested in Apache traditions, and proud of my Native identity. Several of my paintings are exhibited on the Jicarilla Reservation, where I often go back to visit. I don't have to live there to have a strong feeling of identity. I am part of the third generation of painters from my community and among the Native artists who have embraced contemporary art. And I am also conscious that my life is very different from the people who live there on a permanent basis.

Sometimes it's difficult to belong to a community while pursuing an international career away from that community.

JR: Unlike other artists you have never taught art. You always have taken risks: leaving home at the age of fifteen, getting married very young, having a daughter although you could not be sure you would make a living as an artist, then always counting on the development of artistic activities in Santa Fe and in the Southwest.

DVG: I always managed to make a living as a creative artist. After having acquired my training at the IAIA, I had to leave, to gain my own freedom. I never wanted to teach. I know some very good and famous artists or writers who have done so, for example, Allan Houser or Scott Momaday; but I always perceived teaching as a great risk because I felt it would mean that I would have to sacrifice my own creativity, it would lead me to some sort of artistic routine. Actually, I thought teaching would put me in danger and could transform me into a frustrated artist.

I am convinced that one has to take risks. I remember that when I was a child my father would take me to the plaza in Santa Fe. I looked at the artists selling artifacts to tourists and I thought I might be willing to do that. I felt good there. I could have taken the risk to start like that.

It is true that I got married very early. I followed my first wife on the powwow trail. We had nothing. I became a very young father and I had to assume family responsibilities as a very young man. Then I started exhibiting my work in Santa Fe in collective shows and looked out for small galleries that could help me get a good start. Then I moved on to solo shows in famous galleries. My reputation spread very fast. And I always accepted the opportunity to go abroad to acquire a wider experience and to meet with different people.

Although my Apache identity, my interest in Apache rituals, and my attachment to the Southwest landscape are very deeply reflected in my work, I feel free to explore both abstraction and representation. My wife Jill has inspired many of my figurative paintings. Apache crown dancers are recurrent themes, interpreted in many different ways, and my very peculiar and intense landscapes have become very popular.

JR: Have you been influenced by some of the older Native artists that you have met? Do you feel a special bond with the Apache sculptor Allan Houser?

DVG: It has been very inspiring to be part of the artistic creativity fostered by the IAIA over the last decades. The increasing reputation of Indian Market, with the number of crowded openings in important galleries every year, attracting many collectors from outside New Mexico, also helped me to be in touch with older, more established painters. But I always wanted to assert my own identity, without following in the footsteps of other artists.

I don't identify with Allan Houser, who is an Apache artist from a different community, even though I admire his work. I also knew quite well the Navajo artist R. C. Gorman, who was very famous for a while, and exhibited his work in Europe in the 1970s. He was very friendly to me and invited me, with many other young artists, to his home in Taos. He had his own gallery and managed to acquire an international reputation. I also greatly admire the work of Fritz Scholder and T. C. Cannon. I respect them both tremendously because they have broken new ground in the artistic world. They were very different, Fritz Scholder so strong and powerful and T. C. Cannon so gifted and so fragile. Somehow Cannon's untimely death was not surprising.

Being part, as a junior artist, of the ebullient atmosphere of the New Mexico art scene, encouraged by the recognition of non-Indian collectors, has been extremely stimulating. But I always remained fiercely independent.

JR: You have never been an activist, or a militant. How do you account for that independence that seems to have kept you apart from some of the most significant, spectacular collective political assertions of Indian identity?

DVG: Most militants are mixed-bloods, like John Trudell. They are angry and they feel militancy is going to quench their thirst for recognition. I agree with Scott

Momaday, who says that identity is not linked with blood quantum and I don't feel the need to express my Indian identity through political activism.

Art is another medium through which one can express faithfulness to one's roots or to one's natural environment. My identity is freely reinterpreted in my way of life as a New Mexican artist and in my paintings. And I keep looking for new outlets for my work, in the Southwest and beyond, abroad, for example, where my work has been exhibited and collected.

JR: What are your current projects?

DVG: I have had a recent exhibition in Paris (fall of 2008). I now have a number of European collectors and I know I can work there as an emissary of Native culture. In Santa Fe I have a new studio where I work intensely, always in my own spirit of independence. I don't want to be pigeonholed by my culture. I know, through the feedback I get both from Southwestern and European collectors that my paintings can have a universal appeal. This is what I am looking for, as has been the case for Fritz Scholder and T. C. Cannon. I want to keep away from the more commercial galleries and to develop my ability to look to the long term. I just turned fifty, I am at a crossroads and I want to be selective, less prolific, and my main objective now is to control my own creativity to make only pieces that really count.

I am also starting new activities: I am designing guitars for a close friend in the record business. His name is Robbie Robertson and he is preparing to unveil his Broadway-style Native American musical. Robbie Robertson is of Mohawk ancestry and he, like myself, is both committed to his Native culture and willing to function in mainstream society. Both music and art remain my constant passions.

Darren Vigil Gray's paintings are in leading private collections and in the permanent collections of several museums, including the Wheelwright Museum (Santa Fe, New Mexico), the Institute of American Indian Arts (Santa Fe, New Mexico), and the Denver Art Museum.

He had a major retrospective exhibition at the Wheelwright Museum in 2002. Over the last few years, his work has been exhibited in various galleries (Gerald Peters Gallery, Santa Fe) and museums in the United States and abroad.

2009: Museum Works Galleries (Robert Casterline), Santa Fe and Aspen, Colorado.

2008: (May/June), Collective Show, *Go West*, Gallery Orenda, Paris, France; (September/October), *Visages and Visions: Generations Santa Fe*, with N. Scott Momaday, Gallery Orenda, Paris, France.

2007: Los Angeles Art Show, Barker Hangar, Santa Monica, California; *Cherishing the Muse*, LewAllen Contemporary, Santa Fe, New Mexico.

2006: *Diptychs*, LewAllen Contemporary, Santa Fe, New Mexico.

2005: *Untamable Forces*, LewAllen Contemporary, Santa Fe, New Mexico.

2004: *Contacting My Myth*, Peyton-Wright Gallery, Santa Fe, New Mexico; *One Man Show*, Durango Film Festival, Durango, Colorado.

2003: *We Are Still Here with the Mountains*, group of six Apache painters and sculptors, the Hubbard Museum of the American West, Ruidoso, New Mexico.

2002: *Common Ground*, group exhibition, Tucson Museum of Art, Tucson, Arizona; *Still Humming Thunder*, Peyton-Wright Gallery, Santa Fe, New Mexico; *Counterclockwise / 20-Year Retrospective*, Wheelwright Museum, Santa Fe, New Mexico.

2000: *Let Us Have a Blue Day*, Peyton-Wright Gallery, Santa Fe, New Mexico.

CHAPTER TWELVE

Jill Momaday, actress, model, and former chief of protocol, state of New Mexico

Jill Momaday (Kiowa/Cherokee), actress and model, was chief of protocol of the Department of Cultural Affairs in the team of Bill Richardson, governor of the state of New Mexico until the end of 2010. In that capacity, she became the face of New Mexico in many elegant forums and artistic venues. Her slim figure and delicate features have become a symbol of Native beauty and the diversity of the Southwest.

Being a famous writer's daughter and a talented painter's wife as well as a devoted mother of two girls, she has been striving with a multiplicity of roles. Lately her personal and professional responsibility has increased. Her creative pull is strong and she reflects here on what has made her career and shaped her life and on what could enrich it even more.

Our frequent conversations usually took place in Santa Fe in August, as she was preparing to be events coordinator of many important happenings during Indian Market. In August 2009 she had also accepted the role of model for a fund-raising fashion show organized by trendy Native designers on Allan Houser's estate.[1]

Joëlle Rostkowski: You have studied fine arts at the University of Arizona and French studies at the Sorbonne. You have exercised your creativity in various fields: cinema, theater, modeling, and communication. Your beauty has inspired filmmakers, photographers, and painters, including your husband. Your elegance and background have led to your becoming a contemporary image of the "Indian Princess." How do you feel about that?

Jill Momaday: I have always been the face of something. There has always been a certain idea people look at me for, whether it be filmmakers, photographers, or politicians. I was on the stage as a child and I went out at a very early age to New York, where I became a model.

Jill Momaday *(Photo by Nicolas Rostkowski)*

I realized very quickly that modeling was a harsh, cutthroat environment. It was very pleasant to be nineteen and to live in New York. And it was definitely a time of self-discovery. But living in a big city was a challenge and I felt different from the people around me. I was the only Native girl, although I didn't realize what it meant at the time. I felt closed in. There was no open space, no sky, no light, no land. My spirit was cut off from everything that fed me as a creative being.

The modeling industry is a very cruel environment in which young girls are harshly used without any concern for their inner self. Although I went through the motions, I slowly realized I was sacrificing too much to make a career in such conditions. And I decided to come back to New Mexico.

That experience did not deter me from wishing to discover the world. I decided to go for a year to Paris, where I led a bohemian life. I enjoyed the energy of the French capital, its artistic life. Strangely enough, so far away from home, in an urban environment, I didn't feel closed in. I would walk and walk. It fed me. Everything was so new. I felt the city was vital, boiling with energy, as if it were on fire. I would get close to all kinds of different people, some very posh, some homeless. Nothing was closed off. I experienced the extremes that the city had to offer.

Of course, in the end, I felt homesick again. It was time to come back, to check back with my family, with the Southwestern environment I was familiar with. I wanted to move mountains and change the world. My possibilities seemed endless.

JR: Back in New Mexico you embarked on an acting career that led you to work with famous directors such as Sam Shepard and Oliver Stone. Did you enjoy being an actress?

JM: I had the opportunity to participate in many different projects. I played in the adaptation of Tony Hillerman's *Coyote Waits*, directed by Jan Egleson and produced by Robert Redford. I worked with Sam Shepard in *Silent Tongue* and Oliver Stone in *Natural Born Killers*.

I found acting much more interesting than modeling, although the auditions were terrifying, and gave me the impression that I was selling myself. When you really want a part, you can feel insecure because you have to deal with extreme competition and sometimes rejection. But acting can be exciting, exhilarating.

On the whole, it was fun and I learned a lot. I watched the directors and admired their creativity, their skill, and their determination. I enjoyed the atmosphere on the set and got along very well with the crew. Generally speaking, I felt at ease and I managed to engage in easy friendships, to remain on good terms with the directors, in particular Shepard and Stone. When we happen to meet, we embrace, joke, and have a good time.

However I knew very well that, being a Native girl, I would be confined inevitably to a representation of some stereotypical image or role: Indian princess or hooker. The interesting parts were not there. So I decided to quit the business. But I am still acting occasionally if offered the right opportunity.

JR: Family life and family relationships are extremely important for you. You have a strong marriage and you are a devoted mother. You are close to your father and your sisters. You perceive yourself as "the nurturing kind."

JM: Having children, being a mother, made me realize that life can be terribly superficial. You can easily get sucked into the system. You allow people to project things unto you. You become what they think you are. I disliked that sex symbol put on me. Modeling, film, theater can devour you.

My marriage with Darren Vigil has been a passionate adventure. I became his muse. He expressed his own vision of me. Darren has a unique creativity and is terribly focused on his work. We both have very strong personalities and we have tried, with some difficulty sometimes, to develop equally side by side.

Being a mother has meant a lot to me. It has given me a sense of fulfillment and profound happiness. It has been one of the most powerful things I experimented with in my life. And I share a lot with my daughters: dreams, stories, and legends. Our oral tradition lives in our hearts. One day I will take the time to put those stories, dreams, and visions in writing.

My experience as a mother has been and remains very rewarding and enriching. But I know, like all caring mothers, that there are inevitably some moments when women yearn for their self back.

JR: While assuming your multiple roles, publicly and privately, you have also followed your father's work very closely, contributing actively to the development of his foundation, the Buffalo Trust. You have also helped him in the artistic field, in the organization of a recent exhibit in France, for example.

JM: My father is very close to his four daughters. We admire him tremendously and we would do anything to help him in his many different activities. As I live in Santa Fe we are particularly close. His wife Barbara passed away in the fall of 2008 and I do what I can to help him with the organization of his numerous activities.

I have taken care of some events for the Buffalo Trust, a nonprofit foundation working to preserve Native cultures and to foster the transmission of knowledge among generations. The Buffalo Trust is building a campground in southwestern Oklahoma where young Indian people can be exposed to the teachings of elders. It is establishing a cultural center in the Kiowa community of Rainy Mountain, in Oklahoma, where my father has kept close contact.

In the artistic field, I follow his exchanges with cultural units and galleries wishing to exhibit his works. Recently he has had several shows in Paris, where he is particularly well known and has a great visibility due to his position as Artist for Peace for UNESCO. I have been asked to accompany him on some of his trips to Europe, where some exhibitions of Native American art are planned in the near future.

JR: Your activity as chief of protocol of the Department of Cultural Affairs for the state of New Mexico has required a lot of initiative, control, and know-how in the field of communication and politics. You are in the public eye again. You have represented New Mexico and your presence is required in many venues leading to the promotion of important cultural ventures. Is your current image more in tune with your true self?

JM: Many people had told me over the years that I had the right profile to become an ambassador of Native culture and values. I am familiar with the Native art scene and I know I can make things happen in the cultural field.

I am often asked to be event chair at fund-raising meetings. Recently I was asked to be present at an inaugural event to announce that the Kellogg Foundation had approved an important grant to foster American Indian talents through internships and career opportunities.

It's always a pleasure to contribute to raising awareness about American Indians.

Looking back on my current activities, I feel that, when I had the opportunity to work for the state of New Mexico, that job opening came at the right time. I knew that I had accomplished a lot in my private life and needed some exposure to the public eye again. I did not know Bill Richardson. Everything happened very quickly. I had an interview with the first lady and with the governor. They felt right away that I had the right profile and the required qualifications.

I have enjoyed being in a position of high visibility at the state level. I still feel like an ambassador of Santa Fe, an emissary of its cultural life, a mediator between various institutions.

I take advantage of every opportunity to participate in awareness raising, in the organizing of happenings, partnerships. It's a great privilege to be able to contribute to new developments in the artistic and cultural field, and, most of all, to be in the right position to make things happen.

CHAPTER THIRTEEN

Rulan Tangen, dancer and choreographer

Rulan Tangen is a gracious and talented dancer and choreographer who defines herself as a Métis and a nomad. Her creative work is imbued with a strong sense of Native identity, although she was born and brought up in an urban setting. Her choreography is strongly influenced by her Indigenous identity.

In her early twenties she was awarded several championships in traditional pow-wow dances. But her career started before that as a professional ballet and modern dancer in New York. Since then she has reached out to other Native communities throughout the Americas and created a flexible but tightly knit group of dancers whose traditional training is enriched with exposure to modern ballet performances. Her company is called Dancing Earth, Indigenous Contemporary Dance Creations. She lives and works in New Mexico.

This interview took place in 2009 in Santa Fe, just before Indian Market. In New Mexico she feels at home, in tune with many creative people from various walks of life: writers, painters, dancers, singers, potters, and a vibrant international intelligentsia.[1]

Joëlle Rostkowski: Your childhood and education have been marked by what you describe as a rather nomadic life. You have spent more than ten years in New York and you have also traveled extensively around the world. Is there a place that you consider as your home?

Rulan Tangen: Culturally I am very close to Native communities in the Northern Plains and Canada. It's in Canada that I found the first colleagues I decided to work with. We became pioneers exploring new paths in the field of contemporary Indigenous dancing.

Rulan Tangen *(Photo by Larry Price)*

Before creating my own dance company I started off as a traditional dancer. Traditional dancing is very formal and I have been through the training and rituals of Indigenous contemporary dance. Rather early in my career I became a Champion of Northern Plains traditional dance.

I have also an extensive experience of urban life. I spent ten years in New York between the age of sixteen and twenty-six. Although I learned a lot in that stimulating and competitive environment, I felt too far from Nature and from the contact with Native communities. In New York you have to insulate yourself, you are far from Nature and you have to protect yourself from a rather abrasive context. I realize this opinion has a lot to do with my own perception of well-being and happiness. I feel better in Canada, in California and, most of all, in the Southwest.

Santa Fe has become home for me. I like its artistic atmosphere, the visual arts, the community life, the creativity of the people who live in that area and the accessibility of people and institutions. Santa Fe is unique; it's a city where people gather spontaneously on the plaza to listen to music or to dance. In Santa Fe I participate spontaneously and fruitfully in the cultural life, I give a number of performances and manage my company.

I also enjoy traveling, being exposed to other cultures. I have visited a number of foreign countries: Mexico, Brazil, Argentina, where I met other Indigenous groups and where I could recruit and train some of my dancers. I have organized workshops throughout the Americas and it gave me an opportunity to watch promising young dancers and to give them a chance. I invite their own cultural perspectives into our dancing.

JR: Your dance company is organized around a small team of permanent contributors and on the participation of outside artists who join your group occasionally. How can you be both structured enough to be efficient and flexible enough to adapt to various kinds of performance proposals?

RT: Being part of a group is very important. I like solo work, but I also enjoy seeing what other people are doing and building a program around a collective performance. As far as leadership is concerned, I don't really favor hierarchical leadership structure. I rather prefer collective leadership respecting individual personalities. In that respect our group is built around an approach that is totally different from classical ballet companies favoring total submission and sheer formal execution from its members. On the contrary, I try to allow the dancers to reveal their own creativity.

As far as recruiting is concerned, I work with young people who have many abilities: they dance, sing, act. They have several jobs at the same time and can participate occasionally in many different kinds of artistic ventures. This is how I have managed to have a group that is both structured and flexible, with a core of four men and four women.

Everything is Native in our performances: design, costumes, lightning, hairstyle, and makeup. And at the same time we enjoy some hybrid flavor, interwoven philosophies, mixing various Indigenous cultures. We change our repertory each year, depending on the commissions, the grants that we obtain from foundations.

JR: Your choreography has been recognized as a successful and inspiring fusion of modern dance and Native American traditional steps and rhythms. As a groundbreaking artist proposing fresh choreography, embracing Afro-Brazilian music and dance and Latin American influences, is it easy to find sponsors?

RT: It is always difficult to break new ground, to propose something really new. But I had the opportunity to work with of a couple of mentors, who were really pioneers. Raoul Trujillo and Rosalie Jones, for example. Raoul was one of the founders of the American Indian Dance Company and Rosalie was doing a lot of narrative work based upon Native mythology. I worked with both of them, not as a student but as someone who was sharing the same perspective.

My dance company has no founding body. I have to do a lot of grant writing and I do get rather regular support from nonprofit foundations. All that involves a lot of administrative work. As for national grants, they usually require more complex paperwork. Funding is of major importance, but I cannot spend all my time on grant-writing, as I have to keep traveling and teaching. Everything rests on my shoulders.

We have received some support from the IAIA (Institute of American Indian Arts) and, recently, we have obtained funding for a National Grant project. It's the first time a Native contemporary dance company was awarded such sponsorship. We'll be touring the country in 2010 and 2011.

JR: How would you describe your dance company's philosophy?

RT: Through our performances, we want to explore and to share Native perspectives of humanity, to stress our relation to the Earth. Mythology is incorporated into our dancing themes and we are very concerned about the environment.

All those concerns have a direct impact on our functioning. Our costumes are made with recycled material. We incorporate green energy into our productions. We want to convey an Indigenous worldview, to stress our determination to do all that's possible to live in balance with the environment.

Our message tends to be intertribal. The dancers would be recognizable through their hairstyle, whether it is Mohawk, Apache, or Lakota, or others. We would be mixing elements from three or four tribes and weave them all together in a performance that would express our common concerns, our determination to cling to our roots, to remain faithful to our cultures.

RULAN TANGEN AND DANCING EARTH

. . . Tangen takes as inspiration aboriginal origin stories from all sides of the globe. She choreographs these interspecies and interplanetary stories, made vivid with costuming, hairstyles, and body paint. These are not sacred traditional dances, though she is influenced by the forms and movement language of traditional Native dance. Green is the theme of this new production by her company—ecological and cultural sustainability, seen through the intersection of ritual, culture, and ecology . . .

Concurrent with the Olympian efforts involved in developing a dance company, Tangen dealt with and overcame a serious cancer, using the same will, focus, intelligence, and community support that has breathed life into Dancing Earth. Out of the health challenge came inspiration for a specific viewpoint in an aspect of a creation story—recreation from a dark place—performed by the artists who became the core of her company, which was formally created in 2004.

Tangen writes in an essay for a forthcoming anthology by indigenous dance pioneers, that, in her company, "We go through a series of exercises of unmaking, or returning the body into raw instinct. . . . We seek out the movement from the marrow. . . . Then, by incorporation of Indigenous language and sound patterns and philosophies, we start to find rhythms and motions that bring articulation to the primordial ooze." She encourages each member of Dancing Earth to make conceptual and movement-specific contributions to the work . . .

The company goes. . . . The dancers becoming stars, shiny sawdust, a mythic woman who falls from the stars, spiders, caterpillars, a dead-ringer for a scorpion, turtle, bird, rabbit, air, praying mantis, dry earth, water, yucca.

—Janet Eigner
Eigner Dance Reviews, February 2010

CHAPTER FOURTEEN

Robert Tim Coulter, lawyer, founder and director of the Indian Law Resource Center

Robert Tim Coulter (Potawatomi) is an attorney and an enrolled member of the Citizen Potawatomi Nation. He has been instrumental in the development of international law in the field of Indian rights. He was among the first Native lawyers who came to Geneva, Switzerland in the 1970s, to ask for the recognition of Indian Nations and the human rights of Indigenous peoples by the United Nations. A number of Indigenous delegations were then following in the footsteps of Deskaheh, the first American Indian who, fifty years earlier, in 1923, came to the League of Nations with his *Red Man's Appeal for Justice*, in which he asked for the recognition of Iroquois sovereignty on the international scene.

Coulter is an idealist-pragmatist. As a lawyer, he has been concerned with standard-setting and seeking remedies in concrete cases of violations of human rights rather than sheer rhetoric.

While he expressed an idealist conviction in the goodwill and visibility of international forums in the field of Indian rights, he also founded, in 1978, in his early thirties, the Indian Law Resource Center, a nonprofit law firm specializing in the concrete defense of Indian rights at the national and international levels.

As an attorney who practices in the fields of Indian law and international human rights, Coulter belongs to the generation of Indian lawyers who, born just after the war, graduated from the best universities in the 1960s (Williams College, 1966; Columbia Law School, 1969) and chose a career in nonprofit organizations in order to reform existing legal doctrines perceived as unfair, lobby for reform, and break new ground in the assertion of Indian rights.

The Indian Law Resource Center has been active for more than thirty years throughout the Americas. It has never accepted government money and it draws its

Robert Tim Coulter in front of Memorial Sphere, Ariana Park, United Nations, Geneva. *(Courtesy of the Indian Law Resource Center)*

financial support mostly from foundations, as well as individuals and Indian nations themselves. It has always contested the fact that the United States can put Indian nations and tribes out of existence at any time by terminating their rights. While it has become a respected and well-established law firm, it has always preserved its cutting edge.

As executive director, Robert Tim Coulter has remained faithful to his convictions and to a certain way of life, a personal balance in tune with his personal values. Trained as a musician, he has played the bass professionally in the Oklahoma City Symphony and, since then, music has always remained an important part of his life: he plays cello, banjo, and guitar.

His law firm, founded in Washington, D.C. because of the proximity to Capitol Hill and government agencies, now has its main office in Helena, Montana, where Coulter chooses to live in a more natural environment near the vast wilderness areas of the Rocky Mountains.[1]

Joëlle Rostkowski: Since 1978, under your leadership, the Indian Law Resource Center has provided legal advice to Indigenous nations throughout the Americas, in the field of human rights, land claims, and environmental protection. Do you remember why and when you decided to become a lawyer? Was it at Columbia University? Did you always want to defend Native American rights?

Robert Tim Coulter: I made the decision just before I graduated from Williams College in 1966. At the time, I did not think of doing legal work for Indian nations, but I felt that a law degree would be useful in a life of political and social activism generally. In law school I learned about and participated in the movement for civil rights, especially equal rights, voting rights, and social equality for African Americans and all races. I also became a trained counselor in regard to the military draft and later in military law. This was the time of the Vietnam War, and I opposed it both as a lawyer and as a folksinger in a coffeehouse just outside Fort Dix, New Jersey. By 1972 I had begun to work in the field of prisoners' rights and prison conditions, but I realized that the skills I had learned were very much needed in the field of Indian law. I soon began to work in that field almost exclusively.

JR: You have been part of the Indian movement that led to the establishment of a Working Group on Indigenous Populations (WGIP), in 1982, by the UN Sub-Commission on Prevention of Discrimination and Protection of Minorities, within the framework of the ECOSOC (Economic and Social Council). You have also taken an active part in the drafting of the Declaration on the Rights of Indigenous Peoples, adopted by the UN General Assembly in September 2007. What led you to believe that the United Nations could give more visibility to Indian claims and contribute to the defense of Indian rights?

RTC: I learned a great deal from working with the Mohawk Nation and the other nations of the Haudenosaunee, or Iroquois Confederacy—the confederacy of Des-kaheh. They insisted that they are true nations entitled to participate in the world community of nations. They suggested that an appeal to the United Nations could be useful in asserting the legal rights of the confederacy. Based on my legal research, I concluded they were essentially correct, and we began to direct correspondence to the United Nations. However, international law was not as favorable or as well developed as we could wish. In 1976, I was asked to help prepare for a major conference of NGOs at the United Nations in Geneva on the topic of discrimination against Indigenous peoples in the Americas. I saw this as a fine opportunity to make a case both for Indian nations and for the need to improve international human rights law. We brought the attention of the United Nations and the world community to the mistreatment of Indian nations in the Americas. My inquiries led me to the conclusion that the best method for seeking recognition of the human rights of Indian or Indigenous peoples was to propose and seek adoption of a declaration of principles or a declaration of rights.

This was the usual first step in the development of a particular area of human rights law. I convened a group of interested Indian leaders and international law experts to discuss this possibility, and the conclusion was that we should begin the effort. I soon drafted a declaration of principles and circulated this among many Indian communities throughout the Americas for comments and suggestions. With the resulting changes, the Declaration of Principles was submitted at the 1977 NGO Conference at the United Nations in Geneva as the central demand or proposal of the Indigenous participants. The declaration included the concepts of group rights, self-determination, rights to environmental protection, and respect for treaties made with Indian nations.

All of these were innovations at the time. However, this effort built upon the study that was being conducted by the subcommission on discrimination against Indigenous peoples.

We contributed to that study and helped to assure that the conclusions reflected the need for recognition of a new category of human rights for Indigenous peoples. By "we" I mean myself, my staff, and the chiefs and other leaders of the Haudenosaunee, many of the Sioux tribes, the Hopi traditional leaders, Seminole traditional leaders, Western Shoshone leaders, and others.

We were aware at the time that the American Civil Rights movement had appealed to the United Nations a generation earlier in about 1952. The women's movement had as well. We had had poor results from appealing to courts in the United States and felt that international attention was a possible means for creating a new normative base—a new set of legal standards about the treatment of Indigenous peoples.

JR: You have been one of the most constant participants to UN debates on Indigenous issues since the 1970s. The Indian Law Resource Center, shortly after the National Indian Brotherhood (NIB) of Canada and the International Indian Treaty Council (IITC),was one of the first Indian organizations to become an NGO (nongovernmental organization) and to gain consultative status with the United Nations Economic and Social Council. Do you recall the long process that led to an Indian representation within the United Nations, and the moment when the concept of Indigenous Peoples became instrumental for the negotiation of Indian rights?

RTC: We had relatively easy access to the UN human rights bodies with the help of the established NGOs in Geneva and New York. We were somewhat different because of the seriousness and extent of our demands and goals. We made oral statements and submitted written statements often, both to win the creation of the first working group and to present the evidence of the gross violations of the human rights of Indigenous peoples. Soon the Indian Law Resource Center applied for and was granted NGO status. The process was political and depended on a shameful balance between East and West. When we finally won the Working Group on Indigenous Populations, we made it a priority to insist that the working group permit all Indigenous persons to participate freely without having NGO status. This was readily granted, and this became the most active and heavily attended working group in UN history. The concept that Indigenous peoples' representatives need not have NGO credentials took hold in the Human Rights Commission as well, and this later contributed to the creation of the Permanent Forum on Indigenous Issues. I expect that in time Indigenous representatives of actual peoples will have a defined status of some sort in the United Nations, because it has proven to be helpful thus far, even though many individuals who in fact have no actual authority to speak for any Indigenous community have abused the opportunity to participate in the UN meetings.

JR: You have been very steady in the defense of self-determination and sovereignty of Indian nations. But you have made clear, on several occasions, the distance between the Indian Law Resource Center and the position of some more radical Indian activists also present in Geneva. Was it difficult to reconcile points of dispute with governments but also to obtain a consensus among the great variety of sometimes disparate nongovernmental organizations on the final text of the Declaration on the Rights of Indigenous Peoples?

RTC: Other groups in Geneva were not more radical, but they often had positions that were not justifiable, useful, or likely to succeed in our opinion. I, and the Indian Law Resource Center, represented the Haudenosaunee or Six Nations Confederacy, some of the Sioux tribes from time to time, and a number of other Indian nations. Our positions were dictated or guided by these Indian governments. Within three years of the creation of the working group, it became clear that it was no longer possible to have consensus among the Indigenous participants. Most of the participants were not Indian or Indigenous governments responsible to their nations.

In contrast, we only represented or worked with legal representatives of actual Indian nations at the United Nations. Naturally it was extremely difficult to persuade states that we deserved respect for our rights, but our steady presentation of evidence and sound argument (not just by me and my organization but many people) in time brought about astonishing changes in the behavior of states and wide agreement among states about most of the main principles of the draft declaration that was produced by the working group.

JR: You have written that the Declaration on the Rights of Indigenous Peoples is a "turning point" and the most significant development in international human rights law in decades. The UN General Assembly adopted the declaration on September 13, 2007, after more than twenty—actually thirty, in all—but twenty years of actual state negotiations. You have devoted an important part of your life, expressed a lot of hope in the process that led to a historical text that prohibits discrimination against Indigenous peoples and defines their rights—both individual and collective—to culture, identity, language, employment, health, and education, while emphasizing their right to maintain their own institutions, cultures, and traditions. The declaration is not binding but provides an ethical frame of reference. Was it a disappointment when you realized that the United States and Canada (together with New Zealand and Australia) would not sign it, at least in 2007?

RTC: Of course, but we continued to work on winning adherence by these governments. As you may know, we felt that the declaration should be adopted by consensus and that further negotiations should be held to reach consensus. The majority of states decided otherwise. The declaration is nevertheless an important development in human rights law. I have described some of the details in my article in the *Idaho Law Review*.[2]

JR: You are now engaged in another international process with the Organization of American States (OAS). You have mentioned in an editorial, entitled "Anniversary of the UN Declaration, more must be done"(17 September 2008 www.indianlaw.org.), that "the OAS is similar to the United Nations and less complex, with 35 Member

Countries, all of them in the Americas, most of them having missions or embassies in Washington, D.C." Do you think that this "All American" project is easier to handle and more useful that the global framework of the UN Declaration on the Rights of Indigenous Peoples? And do you think the Obama administration is likely to be favorable to a strong declaration approved by the OAS?

RTC: I have been involved in the OAS declaration process from the beginning (1989), and it is no doubt of great importance, but it is not more important than the UN declaration. It is of practical importance at this time, because we have the opportunity to persuade the United States to engage meaningfully in the negotiations and to join in a consensus to adopt the American declaration. This would have the same legal significance as supporting the UN declaration so far as international human rights law is concerned and so far as political considerations are concerned. We are working hard to change the U.S. policy and process for dealing with the OAS draft declaration. We have developed a strong political consensus among U.S. Indian nations that the United States should give approval to the UN declaration and should negotiate in good faith on the OAS draft declaration. We don't know what the Obama administration will do. We are in the midst of dialogue and debate with administration officials. In many respects, over the past fifty years, human rights law has developed at the international level despite the lack of approval and participation by the United States. This may prove to be another of those areas or perhaps not. We have met with the new legal advisor to the Department of State, and he is an inveterate advocate for human rights. We shall have to wait until we are older to know the end of this story.

JR: At the national level, the Indian Law Resource Center has been defending the rights of many tribes and nations. What are the current cases and legal issues that seem to you particularly important presently? And what do you think of the fact that the U.S. government announced on December 8, 2009, that it intended to pay $3.4 billion to settle claims that it had mismanaged the revenue in American Indian trust funds for more than a century (Cobell settlement)?

RTC: The Cobell case is one example of the lawless conduct of the United States in regard to Indian nations. We are working to change United States law in many areas where the law is plainly discriminatory toward Indian peoples. We are beginning a national campaign to change many of these laws and legal doctrines. We are also working to improve the way conservation work is done in regard to Indian lands and Indian peoples. The Cobell settlement is probably a good thing. It is almost impossible to judge the actual reasonableness of the settlement, but it is not obviously bad. It seems to establish the conclusion that the United States is obliged to act within the law in dealing with Indians and their property, and that is an important point.

We are working to build on that precept. Equality before the law for Indian nations and Indian individuals is a very important issue in the United States. Indeed, the Cobell case shows that it is still a matter of dispute whether any law applies to the U.S. conduct toward Indians. I think, in time, we will win on this point. I don't mean to sound ironic, but that is the case here and in many countries.

JR: In *Indian Country Today*, dated January 20, 2010, you are quoted as having said that a resolution introduced by Sam Brownback, Kansas representative, introduced to lead to an official apology for the past ill-conceived policies by the U.S. government to the Native peoples, recently signed by President Obama, has remained confidential ("there were no public announcements, no press conferences. No national attention, much less international"). You also add that the Cobell settlement and the Indian health bill have more legal meaning. Do you think that a more widely publicized U.S. apology for policies toward Native peoples might be important, symbolically, on the national and the international scene?

RTC: Yes, it might be. What is most important is that the United States stops doing the things that it is apologizing for. The apology resolution is a silly bit of posturing that has little meaning, obviously. Congress has no apparent intention of changing its ways, and indeed it appears to be oblivious to the fact that it continues to expropri- ate Indian land and money and continues to exert unconstitutional authority over Indian peoples. My hope is that we can get Congress to examine what is wrong with U.S. actions and the many ways in which the United States continues to violate the fundamental rights of Indian nations.

JR: Would you agree to say that, while many problems remain to be solved, a lot of progress has been achieved in the field of Indian rights over the last thirty years and also more recently, during the current administration, at the national and inter- national level?

RTC: A great deal has been accomplished over the past thirty years, no doubt. Indian people are no longer hunted down and shot in South America. Massacres are now relatively infrequent. I am grateful for that, truly. Many countries now accord self-determination to Indigenous peoples and respect (more or less) their land and resource rights. Indigenous peoples now have a permanent right to exist as peoples. These are historic advances in our civilization. Here, in the United States, very little has improved, and much has grown worse. Obama has done nothing of significance yet, but I continue to be hopeful.[3]

I was very pleased when the President announced on 16 December, 2010, the endorsement of the UN Declaration on the Rights of Indigenous Peoples. I feel that in our work for Indian Rights, we can and should use the UN Declaration to evalu- ate laws, to support and advocate for positive legislation and positive government action. What is important is that we now have a worldwide consensus on the UN Declaration—no country opposes it. This means a great deal for its future imple- mentation. It also means that the United States as well as other countries will expect one another to respect those rights. This will add to the respect that countries give to indigenous rights in practice.

> Today, the United States government at last officially endorsed the UN Declaration on the Rights of Indigenous Peoples and joined the inter- national community in recognizing that American Indians and other

indigenous peoples have a permanent right to exist as peoples, nations, cultures, and societies.

The United States is the last of the four countries that voted against the UN Declaration to reverse its position. This endorsement reflects the worldwide acceptance of indigenous peoples and our governments as a permanent part of the world community and the countries where we live. The Declaration on the Rights of Indigenous Peoples is the most significant development in international human rights law in decades. International human rights law now recognizes the rights of indigenous peoples as peoples, including rights of self-determination, property, and culture.

For me, the United States' endorsement of the UN Declaration marks the culmination of over three decades of hard work by indigenous peoples and other members of the international human rights community. In 1976, when the Six Nations and I began the work of drafting and proposing a declaration to be adopted by the United Nations, we did not know that our idea would one day be universally accepted and supported first by indigenous peoples and eventually by the countries of the world. We knew of the terrible inadequacy of legal regimes and the gross violations of indigenous peoples' human rights in most countries. We turned to international law primarily because of the need to overcome and improve national laws and practices and because of the desire to regain a place for indigenous peoples in the international community.

Our work to ensure justice for Indian nations in this country begins in earnest with the United States' endorsement of the UN Declaration. To see the promise of the Declaration become a reality, we must continue to fight for laws, policies, and relationships that take into account the permanent presence of Indian nations in this country, and throughout the world.

The Declaration sets an agenda for the United States and Indian nations to design a reasonable approach to a progressive realization of the duties and responsibilities in it. It serves as a guide for consultations among Indian and Alaska Native nations and U.S. governmental departments and agencies to improve the government-to-government relationship among Indian and Alaska Native nations and the United States . . .

—Robert T. Coulter

CHAPTER FIFTEEN

Kenneth Deer, journalist, educator, and UN Indigenous representative

Kenneth Deer (Mohawk) is a charming and charismatic man, a member of the Bear Clan from the Kahnawake Mohawk community (Quebec), located just across the St. Lawrence River from Montreal.

Kenneth Deer's Mohawk name is Atsenhaienton, which means: "The fire still burns," and it fits him well. He has proven his passionate commitment as a political activist at the local and national level and on the international scene.

For almost twenty years, Kenneth was involved in education at Kahnawake: he was education counselor and high school principal. He eventually became co-chairman of the National Indian Education Council in Canada. In 1992 he broke new ground in the field of journalism when he founded *The Eastern Door*, a weekly newspaper serving his community. In 1999–2001 he served on the board of directors for the Quebec Community Newspapers' Association.

Kenneth Deer has acquired a great deal of visibility on the international scene, particularly with the momentum of the Oka crisis (July 11–September 1990), extensively covered by the media all over the world. Since 1987, he has attended all the meetings of the UN Working Group on Indigenous Populations, and most of the UN-related meetings in Geneva and New York. He had the honor of becoming chairman/rapporteur of the UN Workshop on Indigenous Media in New York in December of 2000.[1]

Joëlle Rostkowski: You have broken new ground as an educator, journalist, and Indian representative at the United Nations. When you look back at your childhood, do you remember feeling like a rebel or a militant?

Kenneth Deer *(Courtesy of Kenneth Deer)*

Kenneth Deer: My childhood and my education are closely linked to Kahnawake. I was born and raised in that community. I was born in my grandmother's house, raised a Catholic, and educated in government schools. I was never sent to a residential school, but, in our "Indian Day Schools," as they were called, we learned nothing about our Mohawk ancestors, nothing about our traditions. I knew I was a Mohawk and what I learned from our culture and our traditions was transmitted locally and through my family.

When I reached high school, I really had a culture shock when I started to attend schools outside our community. I felt different and I remember suffering from prejudice and discrimination. I realized that we were just looked upon as "stupid Indians." We all spoke English and not French even though we were in a majority French-speaking province. My grandmother was a shopkeeper and she spoke French and Mohawk. Many people in our community, at the turn of the twentieth century, could speak Mohawk and French. But because of our men working on high steel where English was the working language and our schools were in English, we became an English-speaking community, French was forgotten, and the Mohawk language lost its importance in many families.

Several members of my family were high-steel workers. My father was a high-steel worker and my brother died on steel. Indian high-steel workers have built high-rise buildings all over the country, including New York State and Manhattan.

People used to say that Indian steelworkers were not afraid of heights. I am not sure. I suppose they learned how to control their fear. Anyway, my brother died on steel and, when he died, it crushed me. I promised myself not to do the same kind of work. But it was difficult to find a job. In the beginning I had to commute to the city of Montreal to work.

As a child, I had dreamt of becoming a physician. But it remained a dream. I also had a strong interest in photography. I worked as an office boy for the Canadian Pacific Railway in the Public Relations and Advertising Department. I enjoyed that line of work but, without a degree, it was difficult to get a promotion.

What changed my life was a job opening as a counselor in the high school in the neighboring community. That job gave me the possibility to develop my potential and to demonstrate my dedication to Mohawk education.

Throughout my youth I have been searching for my identity. I was not a rebel, but I didn't know who I was or what I wanted to be. My parents didn't teach me our native language. They thought that learning Mohawk wasn't going to help me find a job. I was raised a Catholic. I even was an altar boy. But I didn't relate to the church. The Mass was said in Latin. I didn't understand the words pronounced in the church nor the deeper meaning of the rituals and beliefs. I began to wonder why I was there. So I began searching for answers about my culture and history. I learned bits and pieces by talking to my elders and others who had been steeped in our culture and traditions.

Finally I was interviewed for that job as school counselor and I was lucky enough to get it, although, at the time, I didn't have the proper training. I remember clearly that the man who had interviewed me called later and said: "Are you sitting down? You got the job." I think it was a turning point in my life. I was surprised that I was selected because others had more education than I did. I was told later that I was given a chance because I expressed my motivation simply and sincerely. I just said that I really wanted to help our high school kids and I was convinced I could do it. The other applicants did not express themselves that way.

Now, I had to follow a crash course on counseling offered by the University of Toronto. It was called the Native Social Counsellor Training Program and I was in the very first class of students. They called us "pioneers" at the time and but I think that the new recruits were also in many ways guinea pigs. But it worked for me, although it was a challenge. I was doing guidance counseling for over three hundred Mohawk students, and some non-Natives as well who preferred to deal with me. I enjoyed that responsibility and some kids later told me I changed their lives.

At that time I was also a father. My wife Glenda and I had two children, including one adopted child from Saskatchewan. We had two boys to bring up. I had a full-time job and family responsibilities. In both fields Glenda had a very important role. She supported me and was always at my side, on the national scene and on the international scene.

JR: In the 1970s your community went through a tremendous revolution in the educational field and you were an active supporter of the movement that led to important reforms. What were the most important objectives of those reforms?

KD: Our Indian Way School was founded in 1972 and I supported the creation of that school. It was negotiated between the People of the Longhouse, our traditional government, and the Department of Foreign Indian Affairs in Ottawa. The most important objective was a reappropriation of our culture. We wanted to teach new ways of being Indian. We wanted to save our language, our culture, and our traditions. This school was the first in Canada that was totally operated by Native people. Canada's policy of Indian Control of Indian Education did not come out until the next year.

Next came the Kahnawake Survival School, a full-service high school. We paved the way toward a new approach to Indian education. We had volunteer teachers who started Mohawk-language classes. We organized cultural workshops with elders. We were convinced that the survival of our community depended on controlling our education and on the reconstruction of our worldview. We integrated those priorities in our school curriculum and we gave out our own high school leaving diploma, not a Quebec provincial diploma.

I myself was becoming more knowledgeable through contacts with our elders and cultural center workshops. I went through a process that led me to rediscover our traditions and our religion. I joined the Longhouse. I started getting involved in clan meetings and ceremonies. I changed my name and became Atsenhaienton. I enjoy saying, tongue in cheek, that I am a "born-again pagan." And my wife went through the same process. She is a Mohawk immersion language teacher.

I like to say that I am a role player and not a leader. I helped organize the First Nations Education Council in Quebec in order to influence the political process. I became co-chair at the National Indian Education Council. I always wanted the movement to control education to spread to other communities and for government to properly fund our education.

JR: You also had a very important role as the founder of a new newspaper, *The Eastern Door*, and became a well-known editorialist. What led you to get involved in journalism?

KD: Historically, our Haudenosaunee Confederacy included the Mohawk, Cayuga, Oneida, Onondaga, Seneca, and (later) the Tuscarora. The Mohawk were the farthest east in the confederacy so they became known as The Keepers of the Eastern Door. As Kahnawake is the farthest east of the Mohawk communities, I chose that name, *The Eastern Door*, for our weekly newspaper, which is community-based.

I started *The Eastern Door* in 1992 because there was no information in mainstream media on Kahnawake or on matters of interest to us. Most information in the mainstream was generally sensationalist and inaccurate. We needed a platform of information our community could depend on for accurate and balanced news and information. We started from scratch with a small team of volunteers, a lot of dedication, hard work, and the determination to provide a well-documented and relevant source of information.

I was publisher and editor-in-chief of *The Eastern Door* for sixteen years. It's a weekly publication, very well known in the area, considered as an important and trusted source of news. *The Eastern Door* is a member of the Quebec Community Newspapers Association, the Canadian Community Newspaper of Commerce, and the Native American Journalists' Association.

I enjoyed very much my work as editor-in-chief of *The Eastern Door*, and the newspaper won many awards. But, when I realized that I had to devote more and more time to representing the interest of our Nation on the international scene, I decided to interrupt my career as a journalist.

JR: Your involvement on the international scene goes back to the late 1980s. You quickly understood UN mechanisms and became a familiar figure among the NGOs and UN representatives who played a key role in the movement that led to the Declaration on the Rights of Indigenous Peoples. What was your motivation when you decided to attend the meetings of the UN Working Group on Indigenous Populations in Geneva?

KD: In the late 1980s, our Longhouse hired me to coordinate our Nation Office and asked me to go to Geneva to attend the Working Group on Indigenous Populations (WGIP). I knew about the debates on the international scene and I was already familiar with a number of Indian nongovernmental organizations (NGOs), including the International Indian Treaty Council and the Indian Law Resource Center.

I traveled to Geneva for the first time in 1987. I was carrying my Haudenosaunee passport, symbol of our sovereignty, and the Swiss authorities accepted it. At the United Nations, Tim Coulter, director of the Indian Law Resource Center, had to sign us in because we were newcomers at the working group and didn't have the proper accreditation yet.

I was kindly asked to participate in the preparatory meeting of the working group. I had the opportunity to work with Indian representatives from all over the world, including Dalee Sambo, Jim Anaya, Tim Coulter, Ted Moses, and others. I must say that I mostly sat and listened the first time. When I went back home, I gave my people a full report on UN debates.

I never thought I would go to Europe. I felt anxious because I didn't speak any foreign language. I didn't realize everybody would make an effort to speak English to me and help me understand UN procedures.

As I was discovering our negotiations at the UN, our community was going through a crisis. Several months before the Oka crisis, the political situation had been deteriorating. The cigarette stores had been raided because of alleged smuggling. Everybody was armed. I reported some of those problems at the United Nations, where I quickly got to know some of the major players. It caused ripples at home.

In 1990 the Oka crisis broke out. The conflict was complex. It was mostly based upon a long-standing land conflict opposing the city of Oka and the Mohawk community of Kanesatake. A land claim initiated by the Mohawk to obtain restitution of that ancestral land had been rejected in 1986. What spurred the confrontation was the fact that Oka's mayor, Jean Ouellette, announced that the city would expand a golf course and residential development on that land, which included a Native sacred grove and burial ground.

I knew the "Warriors" were ready for a fight. They were armed and were khaki-clad and bandanna-masked. They blocked access to the area. Our people at Kahnawake, in solidarity with Kanesatake, blockaded the Mercier Bridge between the island of Montreal and the south shore suburbs. The police were moving in. The people in Montreal were upset because the regular traffic was blocked. When a policeman was shot and killed, the Canadian Armed Forces were called in and it became quite serious. I was asked to be a negotiator between the two parties. It was surreal. And it was a terrible responsibility. Negotiations were slow, and the Mohawk women had a crucial role in avoiding an even more dramatic confrontation. In our culture, women are caretakers of the land.

The Oka crisis lasted seventy-eight days. It drew much attention to Indigenous issues in Canada. The mayor of Oka finally cancelled the golf course expansion. But our people didn't get the land back. My wife Glenda and I were asked to go to Geneva to report on the Oka crisis before the Working Group on Indigenous Peoples. When I did so, I got a standing ovation and it was the beginning of a long friendship with Dr. Erica Irene Daes, who was the chairperson/rapporteur of the Working Group on Indigenous Populations.

From then on, I could become very actively involved in UN procedures. I was coordinator of the Indigenous Caucus of both the WGIP and also the Working Group on the Draft Declaration on the Rights of Indigenous Peoples. I was also chairman/ rapporteur of the UN Workshop on Indigenous Media in New York in December of 2000. It all led to the final adoption of the Declaration on the Rights of Indigenous Peoples by UN General Assembly in 2007. It was a very important event. However, the fact that four countries, including the United States and Canada, refused to sign the declaration, indicates that much more remains to be done.

The Haudenosaunee have always been leaders on the international scene. In the 1920s, Cayuga chief Deskaheh was the first Indian to travel to Geneva, hoping for international recognition of Iroquois sovereignty. He was stopped from speaking to the League of Nations as Great Britain objected because the Haudenosaunee were not members of the league. Canada, who was not a member either, was upset that the Haudenosaunee were acting more like an independent state then it was, as Canada was represented by Great Britain.

The Haudenosaunee returned in 1977 to attend the NGO Conference on Racism against the Indigenous Peoples of the Western Hemisphere. This was a pivotal meeting, which began the movement of Indigenous peoples in the United Nations that led to the adoption of the UN Declaration on the Rights of Indigenous Peoples. All our delegations came to Geneva on our Haudenosaunee passports, a peaceful statement of our sovereignty, which we still continue today.

In 2008, I came to France and obtained a meeting with the Ministry of Foreign Affairs in order to convince French authorities to let us enter their country with our passports. Today we remain active on all fronts. Mohawk Longhouse representatives—men and women—regularly attend the meetings of the UN Permanent Forum on Indigenous Issues, in order to share information and to report on current conditions on our reservations.

The issues between our peoples and the Canadian and U.S. governments still remain unresolved. Efforts to assimilate Indigenous peoples into mainstream society and eliminate our legitimate right to exist as peoples continue to plague us. It seems our destiny to continue to struggle to survive. We must raise our children and our grandchildren to continue the struggle. If we ever stop struggling, then we will disappear.

CHAPTER SIXTEEN

United Nations Declaration on the Rights of Indigenous Peoples

Adopted by General Assembly Resolution 61/295 on 13 September 2007

The General Assembly,

Guided by the purposes and principles of the Charter of the United Nations, and good faith in the fulfilment of the obligations assumed by States in accordance with the Charter,

Affirming that indigenous peoples are equal to all other peoples, while recognizing the right of all peoples to be different, to consider themselves different, and to be respected as such,

Affirming also that all peoples contribute to the diversity and richness of civilizations and cultures, which constitute the common heritage of humankind,

Affirming further that all doctrines, policies and practices based on or advocating superiority of peoples or individuals on the basis of national origin or racial, religious, ethnic or cultural differences are racist, scientifically false, legally invalid, morally condemnable and socially unjust,

Reaffirming that indigenous peoples, in the exercise of their rights, should be free from discrimination of any kind,

Concerned that indigenous peoples have suffered from historic injustices as a result of, inter alia, their colonization and dispossession of their lands, territories and resources, thus preventing them from exercising, in particular, their right to development in accordance with their own needs and interests,

Recognizing the urgent need to respect and promote the inherent rights of indigenous peoples which derive from their political, economic and social structures and from their cultures, spiritual traditions, histories and philosophies, especially their rights to their lands, territories and resources,

Recognizing also the urgent need to respect and promote the rights of indigenous peoples affirmed in treaties, agreements and other constructive arrangements with States,

Welcoming the fact that indigenous peoples are organizing themselves for political, economic, social and cultural enhancement and in order to bring to an end all forms of discrimination and oppression wherever they occur,

Convinced that control by indigenous peoples over developments affecting them and their lands, territories and resources will enable them to maintain and strengthen their institutions, cultures and traditions, and to promote their development in accordance with their aspirations and needs,

Recognizing that respect for indigenous knowledge, cultures and traditional practices contributes to sustainable and equitable development and proper management of the environment,

Emphasizing the contribution of the demilitarization of the lands and territories of indigenous peoples to peace, economic and social progress and development, understanding and friendly relations among nations and peoples of the world,

Recognizing in particular the right of indigenous families and communities to retain shared responsibility for the upbringing, training, education and well-being of their children, consistent with the rights of the child,

Considering that the rights affirmed in treaties, agreements and other constructive arrangements between States and indigenous peoples are, in some situations, matters of international concern, interest, responsibility and character,

Considering also that treaties, agreements and other constructive arrangements, and the relationship they represent, are the basis for a strengthened partnership between indigenous peoples and States,

Acknowledging that the Charter of the United Nations, the International Covenant on Economic, Social and Cultural Rights and the International Covenant on Civil and Political Rights, as well as the Vienna Declaration and Programme of Action, affirm the fundamental importance of the right to self-determination of all peoples, by virtue of which they freely determine their political status and freely pursue their economic, social and cultural development,

Bearing in mind that nothing in this Declaration may be used to deny any peoples their right to self-determination, exercised in conformity with international law,

Convinced that the recognition of the rights of indigenous peoples in this Declaration will enhance harmonious and cooperative relations between the State and indigenous peoples, based on principles of justice, democracy, respect for human rights, non-discrimination and good faith,

Encouraging States to comply with and effectively implement all their obligations as they apply to indigenous peoples under international instruments, in particular those related to human rights, in consultation and cooperation with the peoples concerned,

Emphasizing that the United Nations has an important and continuing role to play in promoting and protecting the rights of indigenous peoples,

Believing that this Declaration is a further important step forward for the recognition, promotion and protection of the rights and freedoms of indigenous peoples and in the development of relevant activities of the United Nations system in this field,

Recognizing and reaffirming that indigenous individuals are entitled without discrimination to all human rights recognized in international law, and that indigenous peoples possess collective rights which are indispensable for their existence, well-being and integral development as peoples,

Recognizing that the situation of indigenous peoples varies from region to region and from country to country and that the significance of national and regional particularities and various historical and cultural backgrounds should be taken into consideration,

Solemnly proclaims the following United Nations Declaration on the Rights of Indigenous Peoples as a standard of achievement to be pursued in a spirit of partnership and mutual respect:

Article 1

Indigenous peoples have the right to the full enjoyment, as a collective or as individuals, of all human rights and fundamental freedoms as recognized in the Charter of the United Nations, the Universal Declaration of Human Rights and international human rights law.

Article 2

Indigenous peoples and individuals are free and equal to all other peoples and individuals and have the right to be free from any kind of discrimination, in the exercise of their rights, in particular that based on their indigenous origin or identity.

Article 3

Indigenous peoples have the right to self-determination. By virtue of that right they freely determine their political status and freely pursue their economic, social and cultural development.

Article 4

Indigenous peoples, in exercising their right to self-determination, have the right to autonomy or self-government in matters relating to their internal and local affairs, as well as ways and means for financing their autonomous functions.

Article 5

Indigenous peoples have the right to maintain and strengthen their distinct political, legal, economic, social and cultural institutions, while retaining their right to participate fully, if they so choose, in the political, economic, social and cultural life of the State.

Article 6

Every indigenous individual has the right to a nationality.

Article 7

1. Indigenous individuals have the rights to life, physical and mental integrity, liberty and security of person.

2. Indigenous peoples have the collective right to live in freedom, peace and security as distinct peoples and shall not be subjected to any act of genocide or any other act of violence, including forcibly removing children of the group to another group.

Article 8

1. Indigenous peoples and individuals have the right not to be subjected to forced assimilation or destruction of their culture.

2. States shall provide effective mechanisms for prevention of, and redress for:

(a) Any action which has the aim or effect of depriving them of their integrity as distinct peoples, or of their cultural values or ethnic identities;

(b) Any action which has the aim or effect of dispossessing them of their lands, territories or resources;

(c) Any form of forced population transfer which has the aim or effect of violating or undermining any of their rights;

(d) Any form of forced assimilation or integration;

(e) Any form of propaganda designed to promote or incite racial or ethnic discrimination directed against them.

Article 9

Indigenous peoples and individuals have the right to belong to an indigenous community or nation, in accordance with the traditions and customs of the community or nation concerned. No discrimination of any kind may arise from the exercise of such a right.

Article 10

Indigenous peoples shall not be forcibly removed from their lands or territories. No relocation shall take place without the free, prior and informed consent of the indigenous peoples concerned and after agreement on just and fair compensation and, where possible, with the option of return.

Article 11

1. Indigenous peoples have the right to practise and revitalize their cultural traditions and customs. This includes the right to maintain, protect and develop the past, present and future manifestations of their cultures, such as archaeological and historical sites, artefacts, designs, ceremonies, technologies and visual and performing arts and literature.

2. States shall provide redress through effective mechanisms, which may include restitution, developed in conjunction with indigenous peoples, with respect to their

cultural, intellectual, religious and spiritual property taken without their free, prior and informed consent or in violation of their laws, traditions and customs.

Article 12

1. Indigenous peoples have the right to manifest, practise, develop and teach their spiritual and religious traditions, customs and ceremonies; the right to maintain, protect, and have access in privacy to their religious and cultural sites; the right to the use and control of their ceremonial objects; and the right to the repatriation of their human remains.

2. States shall seek to enable the access and/or repatriation of ceremonial objects and human remains in their possession through fair, transparent and effective mechanisms developed in conjunction with indigenous peoples concerned.

Article 13

1. Indigenous peoples have the right to revitalize, use, develop and transmit to future generations their histories, languages, oral traditions, philosophies, writing systems and literatures, and to designate and retain their own names for communities, places and persons.

2. States shall take effective measures to ensure that this right is protected and also to ensure that indigenous peoples can understand and be understood in political, legal and administrative proceedings, where necessary through the provision of interpretation or by other appropriate means.

Article 14

1. Indigenous peoples have the right to establish and control their educational systems and institutions providing education in their own languages, in a manner appropriate to their cultural methods of teaching and learning.

2. Indigenous individuals, particularly children, have the right to all levels and forms of education of the State without discrimination.

3. States shall, in conjunction with indigenous peoples, take effective measures, in order for indigenous individuals, particularly children, including those living outside their communities, to have access, when possible, to an education in their own culture and provided in their own language.

Article 15

1. Indigenous peoples have the right to the dignity and diversity of their cultures, traditions, histories and aspirations which shall be appropriately reflected in education and public information.

2. States shall take effective measures, in consultation and cooperation with the indigenous peoples concerned, to combat prejudice and eliminate discrimination and to promote tolerance, understanding and good relations among indigenous peoples and all other segments of society.

Article 16

1. Indigenous peoples have the right to establish their own media in their own languages and to have access to all forms of non-indigenous media without discrimination.

2. States shall take effective measures to ensure that State-owned media duly reflect indigenous cultural diversity. States, without prejudice to ensuring full freedom of expression, should encourage privately owned media to adequately reflect indigenous cultural diversity.

Article 17

1. Indigenous individuals and peoples have the right to enjoy fully all rights established under applicable international and domestic labour law.

2. States shall in consultation and cooperation with indigenous peoples take specific measures to protect indigenous children from economic exploitation and from performing any work that is likely to be hazardous or to interfere with the child's education, or to be harmful to the child's health or physical, mental, spiritual, moral or social development, taking into account their special vulnerability and the importance of education for their empowerment.

3. Indigenous individuals have the right not to be subjected to any discriminatory conditions of labour and, inter alia, employment or salary.

Article 18

Indigenous peoples have the right to participate in decision-making in matters which would affect their rights, through representatives chosen by themselves in accordance with their own procedures, as well as to maintain and develop their own indigenous decision-making institutions.

Article 19

States shall consult and cooperate in good faith with the indigenous peoples concerned through their own representative institutions in order to obtain their free, prior and informed consent before adopting and implementing legislative or administrative measures that may affect them.

Article 20

1. Indigenous peoples have the right to maintain and develop their political, economic and social systems or institutions, to be secure in the enjoyment of their own means of subsistence and development, and to engage freely in all their traditional and other economic activities.

2. Indigenous peoples deprived of their means of subsistence and development are entitled to just and fair redress.

Article 21

1. Indigenous peoples have the right, without discrimination, to the improvement of their economic and social conditions, including, inter alia, in the areas of educa-

tion, employment, vocational training and retraining, housing, sanitation, health and social security.

2. States shall take effective measures and, where appropriate, special measures to ensure continuing improvement of their economic and social conditions. Particular attention shall be paid to the rights and special needs of indigenous elders, women, youth, children and persons with disabilities.

Article 22

1. Particular attention shall be paid to the rights and special needs of indigenous elders, women, youth, children and persons with disabilities in the implementation of this Declaration.

2. States shall take measures, in conjunction with indigenous peoples, to ensure that indigenous women and children enjoy the full protection and guarantees against all forms of violence and discrimination.

Article 23

Indigenous peoples have the right to determine and develop priorities and strategies for exercising their right to development. In particular, indigenous peoples have the right to be actively involved in developing and determining health, housing and other economic and social programmes affecting them and, as far as possible, to administer such programmes through their own institutions.

Article 24

1. Indigenous peoples have the right to their traditional medicines and to maintain their health practices, including the conservation of their vital medicinal plants, animals and minerals. Indigenous individuals also have the right to access, without any discrimination, to all social and health services.

2. Indigenous individuals have an equal right to the enjoyment of the highest attainable standard of physical and mental health. States shall take the necessary steps with a view to achieving progressively the full realization of this right.

Article 25

Indigenous peoples have the right to maintain and strengthen their distinctive spiritual relationship with their traditionally owned or otherwise occupied and used lands, territories, waters and coastal seas and other resources and to uphold their responsibilities to future generations in this regard.

Article 26

1. Indigenous peoples have the right to the lands, territories and resources which they have traditionally owned, occupied or otherwise used or acquired.

2. Indigenous peoples have the right to own, use, develop and control the lands, territories and resources that they possess by reason of traditional ownership or other traditional occupation or use, as well as those which they have otherwise acquired.

3. States shall give legal recognition and protection to these lands, territories and resources. Such recognition shall be conducted with due respect to the customs, traditions and land tenure systems of the indigenous peoples concerned.

Article 27

States shall establish and implement, in conjunction with indigenous peoples concerned, a fair, independent, impartial, open and transparent process, giving due recognition to indigenous peoples' laws, traditions, customs and land tenure systems, to recognize and adjudicate the rights of indigenous peoples pertaining to their lands, territories and resources, including those which were traditionally owned or otherwise occupied or used. Indigenous peoples shall have the right to participate in this process.

Article 28

1. Indigenous peoples have the right to redress, by means that can include restitution or, when this is not possible, just, fair and equitable compensation, for the lands, territories and resources which they have traditionally owned or otherwise occupied or used, and which have been confiscated, taken, occupied, used or damaged without their free, prior and informed consent.

2. Unless otherwise freely agreed upon by the peoples concerned, compensation shall take the form of lands, territories and resources equal in quality, size and legal status or of monetary compensation or other appropriate redress.

Article 29

1. Indigenous peoples have the right to the conservation and protection of the environment and the productive capacity of their lands or territories and resources. States shall establish and implement assistance programmes for indigenous peoples for such conservation and protection, without discrimination.

2. States shall take effective measures to ensure that no storage or disposal of hazardous materials shall take place in the lands or territories of indigenous peoples without their free, prior and informed consent.

3. States shall also take effective measures to ensure, as needed, that programmes for monitoring, maintaining and restoring the health of indigenous peoples, as developed and implemented by the peoples affected by such materials, are duly implemented.

Article 30

1. Military activities shall not take place in the lands or territories of indigenous peoples, unless justified by a relevant public interest or otherwise freely agreed with or requested by the indigenous peoples concerned.

2. States shall undertake effective consultations with the indigenous peoples concerned, through appropriate procedures and in particular through their representative institutions, prior to using their lands or territories for military activities.

Article 31

1. Indigenous peoples have the right to maintain, control, protect and develop their cultural heritage, traditional knowledge and traditional cultural expressions, as well as the manifestations of their sciences, technologies and cultures, including human and genetic resources, seeds, medicines, knowledge of the properties of fauna and flora, oral traditions, literatures, designs, sports and traditional games and visual and performing arts. They also have the right to maintain, control, protect and develop their intellectual property over such cultural heritage, traditional knowledge, and traditional cultural expressions.

2. In conjunction with indigenous peoples, States shall take effective measures to recognize and protect the exercise of these rights.

Article 32

1. Indigenous peoples have the right to determine and develop priorities and strategies for the development or use of their lands or territories and other resources.

2. States shall consult and cooperate in good faith with the indigenous peoples concerned through their own representative institutions in order to obtain their free and informed consent prior to the approval of any project affecting their lands or territories and other resources, particularly in connection with the development, utilization or exploitation of mineral, water or other resources.

3. States shall provide effective mechanisms for just and fair redress for any such activities, and appropriate measures shall be taken to mitigate adverse environmental, economic, social, cultural or spiritual impact.

Article 33

1. Indigenous peoples have the right to determine their own identity or membership in accordance with their customs and traditions. This does not impair the right of indigenous individuals to obtain citizenship of the States in which they live.

2. Indigenous peoples have the right to determine the structures and to select the membership of their institutions in accordance with their own procedures.

Article 34

Indigenous peoples have the right to promote, develop and maintain their institutional structures and their distinctive customs, spirituality, traditions, procedures, practices and, in the cases where they exist, juridical systems or customs, in accordance with international human rights standards.

Article 35

Indigenous peoples have the right to determine the responsibilities of individuals to their communities.

Article 36

1. Indigenous peoples, in particular those divided by international borders, have the right to maintain and develop contacts, relations and cooperation, including activities for spiritual, cultural, political, economic and social purposes, with their own members as well as other peoples across borders.

2. States, in consultation and cooperation with indigenous peoples, shall take effective measures to facilitate the exercise and ensure the implementation of this right.

Article 37

1. Indigenous peoples have the right to the recognition, observance and enforcement of treaties, agreements and other constructive arrangements concluded with States or their successors and to have States honour and respect such treaties, agreements and other constructive arrangements.

2. Nothing in this Declaration may be interpreted as diminishing or eliminating the rights of indigenous peoples contained in treaties, agreements and other constructive arrangements.

Article 38

States in consultation and cooperation with indigenous peoples shall take the appropriate measures, including legislative measures, to achieve the ends of this Declaration.

Article 39

Indigenous peoples have the right to have access to financial and technical assistance from States and through international cooperation, for the enjoyment of the rights contained in this Declaration.

Article 40

Indigenous peoples have the right to access to and prompt decision through just and fair procedures for the resolution of conflicts and disputes with States or other parties, as well as to effective remedies for all infringements of their individual and collective rights. Such a decision shall give due consideration to the customs, traditions, rules and legal systems of the indigenous peoples concerned and international human rights.

Article 41

The organs and specialized agencies of the United Nations system and other intergovernmental organizations shall contribute to the full realization of the provisions of this Declaration through the mobilization, inter alia, of financial cooperation and technical assistance. Ways and means of ensuring participation of indigenous peoples on issues affecting them shall be established.

Article 42

The United Nations, its bodies, including the Permanent Forum on Indigenous Issues, and specialized agencies, including at the country level, and States shall promote respect for and full application of the provisions of this Declaration and follow up the effectiveness of this Declaration.

Article 43

The rights recognized herein constitute the minimum standards for the survival, dignity and well-being of the indigenous peoples of the world.

Article 44

All the rights and freedoms recognized herein are equally guaranteed to male and female indigenous individuals.

Article 45

Nothing in this Declaration may be construed as diminishing or extinguishing the rights indigenous peoples have now or may acquire in the future.

Article 46

1. Nothing in this Declaration may be interpreted as implying for any State, people, group or person any right to engage in any activity or to perform any act contrary to the Charter of the United Nations or construed as authorizing or encouraging any action which would dismember or impair, totally or in part, the territorial integrity or political unity of sovereign and independent States.

2. In the exercise of the rights enunciated in the present Declaration, human rights and fundamental freedoms of all shall be respected. The exercise of the rights set forth in this Declaration shall be subject only to such limitations as are determined by law and in accordance with international human rights obligations. Any such limitations shall be non-discriminatory and strictly necessary solely for the purpose of securing due recognition and respect for the rights and freedoms of others and for meeting the just and most compelling requirements of a democratic society.

3. The provisions set forth in this Declaration shall be interpreted in accordance with the principles of justice, democracy, respect for human rights, equality, non-discrimination, good governance and good faith.

In memory of Deskaheh

Deskaheh, a Cayuga chief and member of the Sour Springs Longhouse, spokesman of the Six Nations of the Grand River Land, near Brantford, Ontario, brought the cause of Iroquois sovereignty to the League of Nations, in Geneva, in 1923.[1] He was known for his negotiating ability and his oratorical skills and, in Geneva, he inspired much sympathy and respect as a patient and unflappable spokesman.

During the years following the First World War, the commitment of the League to the protection of "small nations" reinforced Deskaheh's expectations. With his *Redman's Appeal for Justice*, he managed to inspire much sympathy. He secured the assistance of humanitarian and support groups and was encouraged by several member governments.

Although Deskaheh did not succeed in being heard by the League of Nations, his mission is still remembered on the international scene. It has been a source of encouragement for the Native American NGOs who came to the United Nations in Geneva in the 1970s, 1980s, and 1990s to defend "indigenous rights."

"My heart is broken," wrote Deskaheh before leaving Geneva. He was desperate to think that he had failed, but it set his mind at rest to think that his mission would not be forgotten. In his last speech in March 1925 he declared: *"it has gone into the records where your children can find it when I may be dead."*[2]

Deskaheh *(Courtesy of Centre d'iconographic penevoise-BGE)*

Notes

PREFACE. TRAGIC WISDOM AND SURVIVANCE

1. Aileen Moreton-Robinson, "Terra Nullius and the Possessive Logic of Patriarchal Whiteness: Race and Law Matters," in Rosemary Hunter and Mary Keyes, eds., *Changing Law: Rights, Regulation and Reconciliation* (Aldershot and Burlington: Ashgate, 2005), p. 124.

2. Gerald Vizenor, "Crows Written on the Poplars: Autocritical Autobiographies," in B. Swann and A. Krupat, eds., *I Tell You Now: Autobiographical Essays by Native American Writers*, pp. 99–110 (Lincoln: University of Nebraska Press, 1987), p. 105.

3. Gerald Vizenor, *Manifest Manners: Narratives on Postindian Survivance* (Lincoln: University of Nebraska Press, 1994), p. 63.

4. Quoted in Louis Owens, "The Last Man of the Stone Age: Gerald Vizenor's *Ishi and the Wood Ducks*," in A. Robert Lee, ed., *Loosening the Seams: Interpretations of Gerald Vizenor* (Bowling Green: Bowling Green State University Press, 2000), p. 236.

5. Ibid., p. 237.

INTRODUCTION. FROM FORGOTTEN AMERICANS TO INDIGENOUS RIGHTS

1. Barack Obama, White House Tribal Nations Conference, November 5, 2009.

2. Vine Deloria Jr., Introduction to *American Indian Policy in the Twentieth Century* (Norman: University of Oklahoma Press, 1985), p. 6.

3. Joyotpaul Chaudhuri, "American Indian Policy, an Overview," in Vine Deloria Jr., ed., *American Indian Policy in the Twentieth Century* (Norman: University of Oklahoma Press, 1985), p. 31.

4. Kenneth Lincoln, *Native American Renaissance* (Berkeley: University of California Press, 1983).

5. Alan Velie, *Four Native American Literary Masters: A Study of James Welch, Scott Momaday, Gerald Vizenor, and Leslie Silko* (Norman: University of Oklahoma Press, 1982).

6. Nancy J. Peterson, "Introduction: Native American Literature: From the Margins to the Mainstream," *Modern Fiction Studies* 45, no. 1 (Spring 1999): 1–9.

7. Claire Charters and Rodolfo Stavenhagen, eds., *Making the Declaration Work: The United Nations Declaration on the Rights of Indigenous Peoples* (Copenhagen: IWGIA, 2009).

8. Steven Tullberg, "Indigenous Peoples: Self-Determination, and the Unfounded Fear of Secession," *European Review of Native American Studies* 9, no. 2 (1995), special issue on the United Nations, edited by Joëlle Rostkowski.

9. Indian and Northern Affairs, Office of the Honourable John Duncan.

10. State.gov/documents.

11. Ibid. *Announcement of US Support for the United Nations Declaration on the Rights of Indigenous Peoples* (state-gov/p/io).

12. James Anaya, UNSR Website, Geneva, December 17, 2011.

13. Andrea Carmen, Yaqui Nation, Executive Director of the International Indian Treaty Council, in *Indian Country Today*, January 5, 2011.

14. Indian Law Resource Center, Editorial, December 16, 2011.

15. Julian Burger, "Making the Declaration Work for Human Rights in the UN System," in Claire Charters and Rodolfo Stavenhagen, eds., *Making the Declaration Work*: *The United Nations Declaration on the Rights of Indigenous Peoples* (Copenhagen: IWGIA, 2009), p. 311.

16. Vine Deloria Jr., Preface to *American Indian Policy in the Twentieth Century* (Norman: University of Oklahoma Press, 1985), p. 5.

CHAPTER ONE. N. SCOTT MOMADAY, POET, NOVELIST, PAINTER, AND UNESCO ARTIST FOR PEACE

1. Charles L. Woodard, *Ancestral Voice: Conversations with N. Scott Momaday* (New York: Barnes and Noble, 1991), introduction, p. ix.

2. I met N. Scott Momaday in 1986 as I was finishing a book entitled *Le renouveau indien aux États-Unis* (Native American Renaissance) based upon my PhD dissertation for the Sorbonne. It was my first interview of the Pulitzer Prize winner, and founder and president of the Buffalo Trust. Since then, we have worked together on several projects and met almost every year, in academic forums or at UNESCO, where he was appointed Artist for Peace in 2004.

CHAPTER TWO. SUZAN HARJO, POLICY ADVOCATE, JOURNALIST, ESSAYIST, AND POET

1. I have known Suzan Harjo for several years. I met her at the National Museum of the American Indian, when I was invited with other scholars, including the French historian Nelcya Delanoë, the writer Gerald Vizenor, and the Canadian painter Robert Houle, to compare the NMAI and the new Musée du Quai Branly, inaugurated by President Chirac in Paris in June 2006. I was very impressed when I realized that Suzan Harjo had been instrumental in bringing about so many sociopolitical changes in American Indian affairs, important legal reforms I had learned about as a historian. Those historical landmarks were illuminated by her personal accounts of the work accomplished by a number of committed people behind the scenes.

CHAPTER THREE. RICHARD WEST, LAWYER AND FOUNDING DIRECTOR OF THE NATIONAL MUSEUM OF THE AMERICAN INDIAN

1. I met Richard West in 1992 when UNESCO launched a project to commemorate the "discovery" of America by Christopher Columbus in 1492. It then became politically correct to call that commemoration the "Encounter between Europe and the New World." On the international scene, it became an opportunity to reflect on the circumstances and consequences of this interchange between peoples and cultures. I was then coordinating the book *Destins croisés, cinq siècles de rencontres avec les Amérindiens* (*Destinos Cruzados, cinco siglos de Encuentros con los Amerindios, Siglo Veintiuno Editiones*) (Albin Michel/UNESCO). Richard West wrote an essay about his own identity, as a "man between two Worlds," and about his fervent hope to establish a "museum different" in Washington.

CHAPTER FIVE. SVEN HAAKANSON, DIRECTOR OF THE ALUTIIQ MUSEUM, KODIAK, ALASKA

1. I met Sven Haakanson at a symposium at the Quai Branly Museum, organized by the American Indian Workshop, a European research group in Native American studies. Since then, thanks to Gwenaële Guigon, who was documenting and reorganizing Inuit collections at the Quai Branly Museum, I have followed his career and the results of his collaborative efforts.

2. Dominique Desson, *Masked Rituals of the Kodiak Archipelago*. Unpublished PhD dissertation, University of Alaska Fairbanks, 1995.

3. Sarah Froning Deleporte, "Trois musées, une question, une république," in *La fracture coloniale*, Nicolas Bancel et al. (Paris: Le Découverte, 2005), pp. 105–111.

CHAPTER SIX. VERONICA TILLER, HISTORIAN, CONSULTANT, AND WRITER

1. I met Veronica Tiller in the 1980s, at a symposium organized in Italy by the American Indian Workshop, the first interdisciplinary European research group on Native American studies. Since then we have met regularly and cooperated on many projects, at the academic level and, lately, within the framework of NTEC (National Tribal Environment Council) and UNESCO.

CHAPTER SEVEN. ERMA VIZENOR, TRIBAL CHAIR, WHITE EARTH RESERVATION, MINNESOTA

1. I met Erma Vizenor on White Earth Reservation and have followed her career over the last few years. She has faced a lot of political conflicts and economic problems with remarkable courage and forbearance. The new White Earth Constitution marks the beginning of a new approach to politics in her community.

CHAPTER EIGHT. LOUISITA WARREN, ELDER OF SANTA CLARA PUEBLO

1. Dave Warren introduced me to his mother when I was doing research on the history of Christian missions on Indian land (Pueblos and Plains Indians). My

husband and I have known Dave Warren's family for many years. We had the pleasure to attend Santa Clara's annual feast day together. In 2009 we saw Dave dancing and singing with his son Alvin. I met Dave at UNESCO on several occasions and we have over the years shared ideas on Native spirituality and on the development of contemporary Indian art through institutions such as the NMAI.

CHAPTER NINE. TONY ABEYTA, PAINTER AND SCULPTOR

1. In the course of my research into the Native American art scene, I have watched the development of Tony Abeyta's career and admired his capacity to acquire a national and an international reputation as a painter. I was a frequent visitor of his gallery in Taos and a witness of his success in Washington in 2004, when his multi-panel painting *Anthem* was chosen as the official image of the grand opening of the NMAI and displayed on banners along the mall. Since then I have discovered his extraordinary ability to adapt to a variety of cultural and artistic contexts.

CHAPTER TEN. DAVID BRADLEY, PAINTER AND SCULPTOR

1. I have followed David Bradley's work for many years since the 1980s, when I was collecting Indian posters for an exhibition planned in various European museums. I found his work striking and interesting from a historical point of view. Since then, Indian posters have been collected and exhibited in various European museums: Musée de l'Homme de Paris, Müseum für Volkerkunde, Musée d'Ethnographie of Geneva (Switzerland). An exhibition of Indian posters, organized at Warsaw University in May 2009, including more recent works, is circulating in Eastern Europe.

2. Gerald Vizenor, "Bradlarian Baroque: The Narrative Art of David Bradley," in *David Bradley: Restless Native, the Journey* (Casper: Nicolaysen Art Museum and Discovery Center, 2008), pp. 1–8.

3. Ibid., p. 7.

CHAPTER ELEVEN. DARREN VIGIL GRAY, PAINTER AND MUSICIAN

1. Darren Vigil Gray was exhibiting his paintings at the 20th Century Fox Gallery in Santa Fe when my husband and I met him in the 1980s. We were then collecting Indian posters for a traveling exhibition planned at the former Museum of Mankind in Paris and the Müseum für Volkerkunde in Vienna. Since then we have watched his success in major galleries in Santa Fe; we have had the opportunity to participate in cultural and artistic happenings together in Europe. At Gallery Orenda in Paris, my husband and I have exhibited his colorful and striking abstract and figurative paintings.

CHAPTER TWELVE. JILL MOMADAY, ACTRESS, MODEL, AND FORMER CHIEF OF PROTOCOL, STATE OF NEW MEXICO

1. I met Jill Momaday when she was living in Paris. I have followed the various activities she has embraced over the years and have admired the delicate balance she has maintained between her career and her personal life, her personal ambitions and her concern for others, her image and her inner self. She keeps extending the scope

of her activities. She has been asked to contribute to some projects and to represent her father on the international scene. She is now specifically working on the Buffalo Trust, founded by her father, which has an office at the Institute of American Indian Arts (IAIA).

CHAPTER THIRTEEN. RULAN TANGEN, DANCER AND CHOREOGRAPHER

1. I met Rulan Tangen in Paris and Santa Fe. She shared with me some of her projects and explained eloquently the specificity of her quest and ultimate ambition: to demonstrate the vitality of Native American dance companies and illustrate Native values and dreams through rhythm, movement, and music. I saw her dancing in Santa Fe and I understood that she could become an ambassador of Native grace in the United States, Canada, and abroad.

CHAPTER FOURTEEN. ROBERT TIM COULTER, LAWYER, FOUNDER AND DIRECTOR OF THE INDIAN LAW RESOURCE CENTER

1. I met Robert Tim Coulter during a symposium on Native American rights organized by the American Indian Workshop (AIW) in Florence. Both of us had a very strong commitment to international negotiations and the standard-setting mission of the United Nations, implemented within the framework of the Working Group on Indigenous Populations set up in Geneva in 1982. We had several opportunities to meet during the Working Group's annual sessions. Robert Coulter wrote a reference article on "Indians on the International Scene (1974–1983)" for the book *Destins Croisés* (Crossed Destinies) that I edited for UNESCO (Paris: UNESCO / Albin Michel, 1992).

2. "The UN Declaration on the Rights of Indigenous Peoples: A Historic Change in International Law," *Idaho Law Review* 45 (2009): p. 529.

3. This conversation took place before Obama's support of the UN Declaration in December 2010. Since then, Robert Tim Coulter has stressed the historic importance of the Declaration and the growing movement of tribes in the United States to change the law to be more in accord with the Declaration. For his latest analysis, see: "The Law of Self-Determination and the United Nations Declaration on the Rights of Indigenous Peoples" in a forthcoming issue of the *Journal of International Law and Foreign Affairs*.

EPILOGUE. IN MEMORY OF DESKAHEH

1. I discovered Deskaheh's mission in the archives of the League of Nations and immediately felt that his memory was worth preserving on the basis of the exclusive information available in many forgotten diplomatic documents. Now that the Declaration on the Rights of Indigenous Peoples has been adopted by the UN General Assembly, he appears as the founding father of Indian diplomacy on the international scene.

2. Akwesasne Notes (ed.), *A Basic Call to Consciousness* (1978), p. 33.

Selected Bibliography

BOOKS AND ARTICLES

Alexie, Sherman

Reservation Blues. New York: Barnes and Noble, Turtleback Books, 1996 (American Book Award).

Conversations with Sherman Alexie, Nancy Peterson, ed. New York: Barnes and Noble, 2009.

War Dances. New York: Grove Press, 2009, 2010 (OEN/Faulkner Award for Fiction).

Allen, Paula Gunn

The Sacred Hoop: Recovering the Feminine in American Indian Traditions. Boston: Beacon Press, 1986.

Anaya, James

Indigenous Peoples in International Law. New York: Oxford University Press, 1996.

Axtell, James

The Invasion Within: The Contest of Cultures in Colonial North America. New York: Oxford University Press, 1985.

Barsh, Russel Lawrence, and James Youngblood Henderson

The Road: Indian Tribes and Political Liberty. Berkeley: University of California Press, 1980.

Berkhofer, Robert F., Jr.

The White Man's Indian: Images of the American Indian from Columbus to the Present. New York: Alfred A. Knopf, 1978.

Berlo, Janet

———, and Ruth Phillips. *Native North American Art*. London, New York: Oxford University Press, 1998. French translation and preface: Nelcya Delanoë and Joëlle Rostkowski, Paris: Albin Michel, 2006.

Bowden, Henry Warner

American Indians and Christian Missions: Studies in Cultural Conflict. Chicago: University of Chicago Press, 1981.

Breinig, Helmbrecht (ed.)

Imaginary (Re)Locations, Tradition, Modernity and the Market in Contemporary Native American Literature and Culture. Tubingen: Stauffenburg Verlag, 2003.

Brown, Dee

Bury My Heart at Wounded Knee: An Indian History of the West. New York: Holt, Rinehart and Winston, 1970.

Brumble, David H.

American Indian Autobiography. Lincoln: University of Nebraska Press, 2008.

Burger, Julian

"Indigenous Peoples: New Rights for Old Wrongs." In *Human Rights*, ed. Peter Davies. London: Routledge / United Nations, 1998.
"How to Make the Declaration Work in the UN System." In *How to Make the Declaration Work*. Copenhagen: IWGIA, 2009.
———, and Frédéric Deroche. *Les peuples autochtones et leur relation originale à la terre, un questionnement pour l'ordre mondial*. Paris: L'Harmattan, 2008.

Castro, Michel

Interpreting the Indian: Twentieth-Century Poets and the Native American. Foreword by Maurice Kenny. Norman: University of Oklahoma Press, 1991.

Champagne, Duane et al. (eds.)

American Indian Activism: Alcatraz to the Longest Walk. Urbana: University of Illinois Press, 1997.

Charters, Claire

———, and Rodolfo Stavenhagen (eds.). *Making the Declaration Work: The United Nations Declaration on the Rights of Indigenous Peoples*. Copenhagen: IWGIA, 2009.

Coulter, Robert Tim

"Using International Human Rights Mechanisms to Promote and Protect Rights of Indian Nations and Tribes in the United States." Indian Law Resource Center, 1 May 2007.

"Anniversary of the UN Declaration: More Must Be Done." Indian Law Resource Center, 17 September 2008.

"The UN Declaration on the Rights of Indigenous Peoples: A Historic Change in International Law." *Idaho Law Review* (October 2009): p. 529.

Daes, Erica Irene

Indigenous Peoples: Keepers of Our Past, Custodians of Our Future. Copenhagen: IWGIA, 2008.

Danziger, Edmund, J.

Survival and Regeneration: Detroit's American Indian Community. Detroit: Wayne University Press, 1991.

Delanoë, Nelcya, and Joëlle Rostkowski

Les Indiens dans l'histoire américaine. Paris: Colin, 1996.

Voix indiennes, voix américaines, les deux visions de la conquête du Nouveau-Monde. Paris: Albin Michel, 2003.

Deloria, Philip, J.

Playing Indian. New Haven: Yale University Press, 1998.

Deloria, Vine, Jr.

We Talk, You Listen. New York: Macmillan, 1970.

Custer Died for Your Sins: An Indian Manifesto. Norman: University of Oklahoma Press, 1969, 1988.

American Indians, American Justice. Austin; University of Texas Press, 1983.

———, ed. *American Indian Policy in the Twentieth Century.* Norman: University of Oklahoma Press, 1985.

———, and David E. Wilkins. *Tribes, Treaties and Constitutional Tribulations.* Austin: University of Texas Press, 1999.

DeMallie, Raymond J.

The Sixth Grandfather: Black Elk's Teachings Given to John G. Neihardt. Lincoln: University of Nebraska Press, 1984.

———, and Douglas R. Parks (eds.). *Sioux Indian Religion: Tradition and Innovation.* Norman: University of Oklahoma Press, 1987.

——— (ed.). *Black Elk Speaks: Being the Life Story of a Holy Man of the Oglala Sioux, The Premier Edition.* Albany, NY, SUNY Press, 2008, with reproductions of the original illustrations by Standing Bear, with new commentary and a revised index.

Diogène

Diogène, Claude Lévi-Strauss, *UNESCO at 60* 54, no. 3 (2007): pp. 5–10.

Eaton, Perry

"From the Artist's Point of View." In *Giinaquq: Like a Face, Sugpiaq Masks of the Kodiak Archipelago.* Fairbanks: University of Alaska Press, 2009.

Erdrich, Louise

Love Medicine. Boston: G. K. Hall, 1984.
The Beet Queen. New York: Henry Holt, 1986.
Tracks. New York: Henry Holt, 1988.
The Bingo Palace. New York: Harper Collins, 1994.
Tales of Burning Love. New York: Harper Collins, 1996.
The Last Report of the Miracles at Little No Horse. New York: Harper Collins, 2001.
The Plague of Doves. New York: Harper Collins, 2008.

Eribon, Didier

Conversations with Claude Lévi-Strauss. Chicago: University of Chicago Press, 1991.

Feest, Christian F.

Native Arts of North America. New York: Thames and Hudson, 1980.
"Repatriation: A European View on the Question of Restitution of Native American Artifacts." *European Review of Native American Studies* 9, no. 2 (1995): pp. 33–42.
——— (ed.). *Indians and Europe: An Interdisciplinary Collection of Essays*. Lincoln: University of Nebraska Press, 1999.
———, and Joëlle Rostkowski. *Indian Posters of North America*. Vienna: Müseum für Volkerkunde, 1982.

Fixico, Donald L.

Termination and Relocation: Federal Indian Policy, 1845–1960. Albuquerque: University of New Mexico Press, 1986.
——— (ed.). *Rethinking American Indian History*. Albuquerque: University of New Mexico Press, 1997.

Gazette des Beaux-Arts

"The Art of the Northwest Coast at the American Museum of Natural History." Claude Lévi-Strauss, 1943.

Gidley, Mick

Edward S. Curtis and the North American Indian. Cambridge: Cambridge University Press, 1998.
Views of American Landscapes, Cambridge: Cambridge University Press, 2007.

Guigon, Gwenaële

———, and Marie Mauzé. "L'art yup'ik au Musée du Quai Branly; trois masques de la collection Robert Lebel." *Gradhiva* 7 (2008): pp. 150–155.

Haakanson, Sven

——— (ed.). *Giinaquq: Like a Face, Sugpiaq Masks of the Kodiak Archipelago*. Fairbanks: University of Alaska Press, 2009.

Harjo, Suzan

"The National Museum of the American Indian: A Promise America Is Keeping." *Native Peoples Magazine* (Fall 1996).

————, and Mateo Romero, *Painting the Underworld Sky: Cultural Expression and Subversion in Art*. Santa Fe: SAR Press, 2006.

Hauptman, Laurence M.

The Iroquois and the New Deal. Syracuse: Syracuse University Press, 1981.

Her Many Horses, Emil

———— (ed.). *Identity by Design: Tradition, Change and Celebration in Native Women's Dress*. Foreword by Richard West. Washington: Smithsonian Institution Press, 2007.

Hobson, Geary

———— (ed.). *The Remembered Earth: An Anthology of Contemporary Native American Literature*. Albuquerque: University of New Mexico Press, 1980.

Hoxie, Frederick E.,

The Campaign to Assimilate the Indian, 1880–1920. Lincoln: University of Nebraska Press, 1984.
Indians in American History. Chicago: D'Arcy McNickle Center, Newberry Library, 1988.

ICOM (International Council of Museums)

Code of Ethics for Museums, Revised Version. Paris: ICOM, 2006.

Kelly, Lawrence C.

The Assault on Assimilation: John Collier and the Origins of Indian Policy Reform. Albuquerque: University of New Mexico Press, 1983.

Krupat, Arnold

Four American Indian Literary Masters: N. Scott Momaday, James Welch, Leslie Marmon Silko, Gerald Vizenor. Norman: University of Oklahoma Press, 1982.
————, and Brian Swann (eds.). *I Tell You Now: Autobiographical Essays by Native American Writers*. Lincoln: University of Nebraska Press, 1987.

Jennings, Francis

The Invasion of America: Indians, Colonialism and the Cant of Conquest. Chapel Hill: University of North Carolina Press, 1975.

Jonaitis, Aldona

Art of the Northwest Coast. Vancouver, University of Washington Press, 2006.

Lévi-Strauss, Claude.

The View from Afar. New York: Basic Books, 1985.
The Way of the Masks. Vancouver: University of Washington Press, 1982.
The Jealous Potter. Chicago: University of Chicago Press, 1988.
Look, Listen and Read. New York: Basic Books, 1997.

Race and History: UNESCO, 1952. New Edition, *Race et histoire (and Race et culture)*. Preface by Michel Izard. Paris: Albin Michel/Edition UNESCO, 2002.

La Pleiade Claude Lévi-Strauss. Œuvres complètes, la Pleiade. Vincent Debaene, Frederick Keck, and Marie Mauzé, (eds.). Paris: Gallimard, 2008.

Lincoln, Kenneth

Sing with the Heart of a Bear: Fusions of Native and American Poetry, 1890–1999. Berkeley: University of California Press, 2000.

Lowe, Truman

Native Modernism: The Art of George Morrison and Allan Houser. Washington, D.C.: Smithsonian Museum of the American Indian (NMAI), 2004.

Madsen, Deborah L.

Understanding Gerald Vizenor. Columbia: University of South Carolina Press, 2009.

—— (ed.). *Native Authenticity: Transnational Perspectives on Native American Literary Studies*. Albany: State University of New York Press, 2010.

Malaurie, Jean

The Last Kings of Thule: With the Polar Eskimos as They Face Their Destiny. New York: Barnes and Noble, 1982.

Ultima Thule: Explorers and Natives in the Polar North. New York: Norton, 1983.

——, with Sylvie Devers (eds.). *L'art du Grand Nord*. Paris: Citadelles and Mazenod, 1981.

Marienstras, Elise

Nous le Peuple. Paris: Gallimard, 1988.*Wounded Knee*. Complexe éditions. Brussels, Paris, 1999.

——, and Bernard Vincent. *Les oubliés de la révolution américaine*. Nancy: Presses universitaires de Nancy, 1991.

——, and Naomi Wulf. *Défense et illustration de la Constitution fédérale des Etats-Unis*, Complexe éditions. Brussels, Paris: 2010.

Mauzé, Marie

"Potlatching as Ever." *European Review of Native American Studies* 9, no. 2 (1995): pp. 25–31.

"Northwest Coast Trees: From Metaphors in Culture to Symbols for Culture." In Laura Rival (ed.), *The Social Life of Trees: Anthropological Perspectives on Tree Symbolism*. London: Berg Publishers, 1998. pp. 233–251.

Arts premiers: le temps de la reconnaissance. Paris: Gallimard, 2000.

"Two Kwakwaka'wakw Museums: Heritage and Politics." *Ethnohistory* 50, no. 3 (2003): pp. 503–522.

——, with Michael Harkin and Sergei Kan (eds.). *Coming to Shore: Northwest Coast Ethnology, Traditions and Visions*. Lincoln: University of Nebraska Press, 2004.

————, and Joëlle Rostkowski. "La fin des Musées d'Ethnographie?" *Le moment du Quai Branly Le Débat* 147 (November–December 1987): [[XXXX]].

Momaday, N. Scott

House Made of Dawn. New York: Harper and Row, 1968 (Pulitzer Prize, 1969).
The Way to Rainy Mountain. Albuquerque: University of New Mexico Press, 1969.
The Names: A Memoir. Tucson: University of Arizona Press, 1976.
The Ancient Child. New York: Doubleday, 1989.
The Man Made of Words. New York: St Martin's Griffin, 1997.
l'Enfant du Soleil. Illustrations Federica Matta. Christopher Moseley (ed.). Paris: Editions du Seuil, 2003.
Atlas of the World's Languages in Danger. Memories of Peoples Series. Paris: UNESCO, 2010.
A Man Made of Visions, A Book of Artist. Paris, ORENDA Art International, 2011.

Murray, David

Forked Tongues, Speech, Writing and Representation in North American Indian Texts. Bloomington: Indiana University Press, 1991.

Museum International (UNESCO and Blackwell Publishing)

Intangible Heritage, No. 221–222.
What Can Art Still Do? No. 244.
Return of Cultural Objects: The Athens Conference, No. 241.
Languages between Heritage and Development, No. 239.
Museums and Cultural Policy, No. 232.
Protection and Restitution, No. 238.

Nabokov, Peter

Where the Lightning Strikes: The Lives of American Indian Sacred Sites. New York: Barnes and Noble, 2007.

Nied, Haline

———— (ed.). *Cultural Rights and Wrongs: A Collection of Essays in Commemoration of the 50th Anniversary of the Universal Declaration of Human Rights*. Paris: UNESCO, 1998.

Ortiz, Alfonso

The Tewa World: Space, Time, Being and Becoming in a Pueblo Society. Chicago: University of Chicago Press, 1969.

Owens, Louis

Other Destinies: Understanding the American Indian Novel. Norman: University of Oklahoma Press, 1992.

Mixedblood Messages: Literature, Film, Family, Place. Norman: University of Oklahoma Press, 1998.

Penney, David

North American Indian Art. New York: Thames and Hudson, 2004.

Philp, Kenneth R.

Termination Revisited: American Indians on the Trail to Self-Determination, 1933–1953. Lincoln, University of Nebraska Press, 1999.

Potts, Michael W.

"Arum Gandhi Shares the Mahatma's Message." *India-West* 27, no. 13 (2002).

Power, Susan

The Grass Dancer. New York: G. P. Putnam's Sons, 1994.
Roofwalker. Minneapolis: Milkweed Editions, 2002.

Powers, Marla, N.

Oglala Women: Myth, Ritual, and Reality. Lincoln: University of Nebraska Press, 1997.

Powers, William K.

Beyond the Visions: Essays on American Indian Culture. Norman: University of Oklahoma Press, 1987.

Prins, Harald E. L.

The Mi'kmaq: Resistance, Accommodation and Cultural Survival. Thompson/Wadsworth Publishing, 1996.
———, William Haviland, Bunny McBride, et al. (eds.). *Cultural Anthropology: The Human Challenge.* Thompson/Wadsworth, 2007.

Prucha, Francis Paul

The Great Father: The United States Government and the American Indians. 2 vols. Lincoln: University of Nebraska Press, 1984.

Rigal Cellard, Bernadette

Le Mythe et la Plume. Paris: Editions du Rocher, 2004.

Rostkowski, Joëlle

"The Struggle for Political Autonomy: U.S. Indians and the United Nations." In Pieter Hovens, (ed.), *North American Indian Studies 2: European Contributions.* Göttingen: Edition Herodot, 1984.
"Deskaheh's Shadow: Indians on the International Scene." *European Review of Native American Studies* 9, no. 2 (1995): pp. 1–5.
La Conversion Inachevée, les Indiens et le christianisme. Preface by Jean Malaurie. Paris: Albin Michel, 1998.

"*The Redman's Appeal for Justice*: Deskaheh and the League of Nations." In Christian Feest (ed.), *Indians and Europe*. Lincoln: University of Nebraska Press, 1987, 1999. pp. 435–453.

Le Renouveau indien aux Etats-Unis, un siècle de reconquêtes. Preface by N. Scott Momaday. Paris: Albin Michel, 2001 (History Prize 2002, French Academy).

"Looking Back: *House Made of Dawn* as the Portrait of a Lost Generation." *QWERTY*.

———, Sylvie Devers, and Jean Malaurie (eds.). *Destins croisés: Cinq siècles de rencontres avec les Amérindiens. Preface by Federico Mayor.* Paris: UNESCO/ Albin Michel, 1992.

Schulte-Tenckhoff, Isabelle

La vue portée au loin: Une histoire de la pensée anthropologique, Le forum anthropologique. Lausanne: Editions d'En Bas, 1985.

Potlatch, conquête et invention: réflexion *sur un concept anthropologique.* Lausanne: Editions d'En Bas, 1986.

La question des peuples autochtones. Brussels: Bruyland, 1997.

"The Irresistible Ascension of the UN Draft Declaration on the Rights of Indigenous Peoples: Stopped Short in Its Tracks?" *European Review of Native American Studies* pp. 5–8.

Silko, Leslie Marmon

Ceremony. New York: Viking Press, 1977.

Storyteller. New York: Seaver Books, 1981.

Almanac of the Dead. New York: Penguin Books, 1991.

Gardens of the Dunes. New York: Simon and Schuster, 1999.

Stavenhagen, Rodolfo

The Ethnic Question: Conflicts, Development and Human Rights. Tokyo: United Nations University Press, 1990.

Strigler, Marie-Claude

La Nation Navajo: tradition et développement. Paris: L'Harmattan.

———, and Sam Begay. *Moi Sam Begay, Homme-Medecine Navajo.* Paris: Indiens de tous pays, 2010.

Sullivan, Lawrence E.

Native Religions and Cultures of North America. New York: Continuum, 2000.

Therrien, Michèle

Printemps inuit: naissance du Nunavut. Indigène, 1999.

———, and Nicole Tersis. *Les langues eskaléoute: Sibérie, Alaska, Canada, Groenland.* CNRS, 2000.

Les Inuits de l'Arctique canadien. CIDEF, 2003.

Tiller, Veronica

The Jicarilla Apache Tribe: A History. Lincoln: University of Nebraska Press, 1992.
Tiller's Guide to Indian Country: Economic Profiles of American Indian Reservations. Albuquerque: BowArrow, 1996.
Culture and Customs of the Apache Indians. Santa Barbara: ABC-CLIO/Greenwood, 2011.

Trout, Lawana

Native American Literature: An Anthology. Lincolnwood: NTC, 1999.

Tullberg, Steven M.

"Indigenous Peoples, Self-Determination, and the Unfounded Fear of Secession." *European Review of Native American Studies* 9, no. 2 (1995): pp. [[XXXX]].

Vickers, Scott B.

Native American Identities: From Stereotypes to Archetype in Art and Literature. Albuquerque: University of New Mexico Press, 1998.

Vizenor, Gerald R.

Griever: An American Monkey King in China. Minneapolis: University of Minnesota Press, 1988 (American Book Award).
Fugitive Poses: Native American Scenes of Absence and Presence. Lincoln: University of Nebraska Press, 1998.
Manifest Manners. Narrative on Postindian Survivance. Albuquerque: University of New Mexico Press, 1994; First Bison Books, 1999.
Bear Island: The War at Sugar Point. Minneapolis: University of Minnesota Press, 2006.
Father Meme. Albuquerque: University of New Mexico Press, 2008.
Native Liberty: Natural Reason and Cultural Survivance. Lincoln: University of Nebraska Press, 2009.
The Shrouds of White Earth Albany: State University of New York Press, 2010.
———— (ed.). *Survivance: Narratives of Native Presence*. Lincoln: University of Nebraska Press, 2008.

Welch, James

Winter in the Blood. New York: Harper and Row, 1974.
The Death of Jim Loney. New York: Harper and Row, 1979.
Fools Crow. New York: Viking Penguin, 1986.
The Indian Lawyer. New York: W.W. Norton, 1990.
Killing Custer: The Battle of Little Big Horn and the Fate of the Plains Indians. New York: W.W. Norton, 1994.
Heartsong of Changing Elk. New York: Doubleday, 2000.

Weston, Mary Ann

Native Americans in the News: Images of Indians in the Twentieth Century Press. Westport: Greenwood Press, 1996.

White, Richard

———, and Patricia Nelson Limerick. *The Frontier in American Culture*. Los Angeles: University of California Press, 1994.

MAGAZINES, REVIEWS, NEWSLETTERS

American Indian Art Magazine, Scottsdale, Arizona. www.aiamagazine.com.

doCIP Indigenous Peoples' Centre for Documentation, Research and Information (Pierette Birraux, director, 14 Avenue de Trembley, CH-Genève, Switzerland (www.docip.org). Established in 1978 to assist Indigenous peoples and scholars. Publishes regular updates (online) on United Nations activities relating to Indigenous peoples.

Ethnohistory, Duke University Press (American Society of Ethnohistory [ASE]), 905 W. Main St., Suite 18 B, Durham, NC, 27701.

European Review of Native American Studies (*ERNAS*), Müseum für Volkerkune, Vienna, Austria and Fasanenweg 4a D-63674 Altenstadt, Germany, Editor in Chief, Christian F. Feest.

ICOM and *ICOM News* (quarterly newsletter of International Council of Museums), Maison de l'UNESCO, 1 rue Miollis, 75 732, Paris Cedex 15 France (secrétariat@icom.musum). ICOM is an international organization of museums and museum professionals committed to the conservation, consultation, and communication to society of the world's cultural heritage, present and future, tangible and intangible. Holds international meetings.

Indigenous Affairs, published twice a year by IWGIA (International Working Group for Indigenous Affairs), Classensgade 11 E, DK-2100, Copenhagen, Denmark (www.iwgia.org).

National Museum of the American Indian (NMAI), Smithsonian Institution, Washington, D.C.

Museum International, UNESCO, Editions UNESCO, 7, Place de Fontenoy, 75352 Paris 07 SP France, www.unesco.org/publishing (Isabelle Vinson, editor in chief). Published by UNESCO since 1948, this publication is a major forum for exchange of information on museum and cultural matters at the international level. It addresses issues relevant to cultural policies, ethics, and museum practices.

Recherches amérindiennes au Québec, 6742, rue Saint Denis, Montréal, Québec, Canada, H2S 2S2 (reamqu@globetrotter.net).

Index of People

General Index

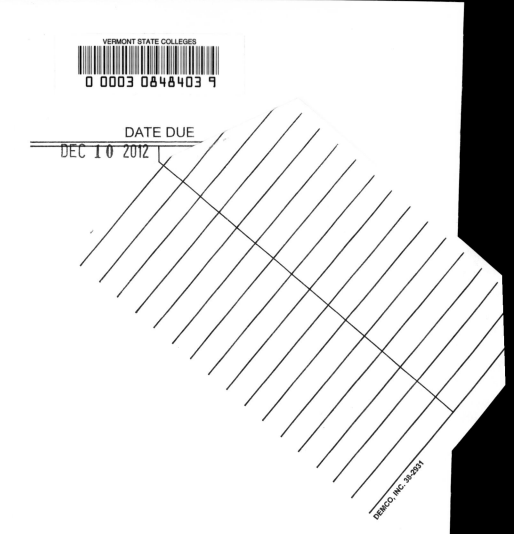

DATE DUE

DEC 1 0 2012

DEMCO, INC. 38-2931